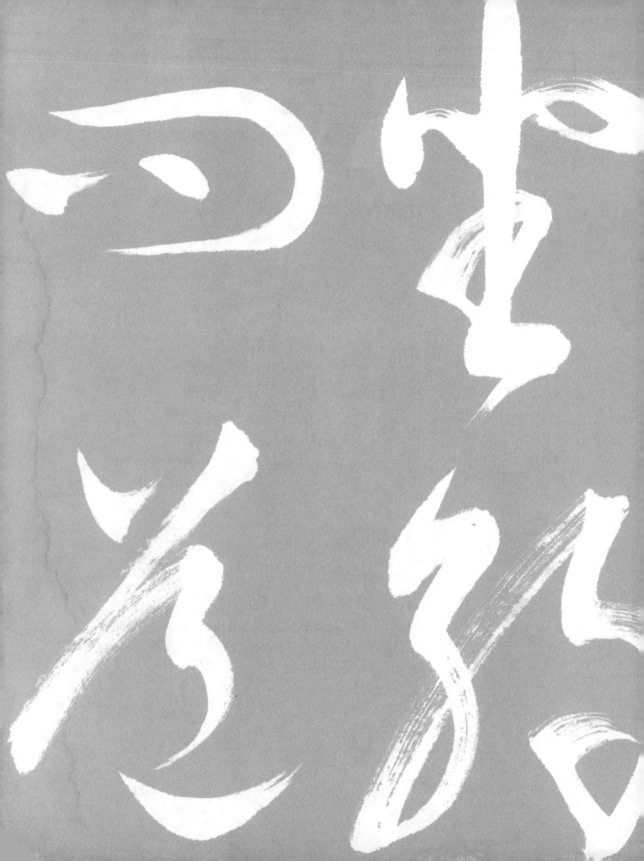

michi

Japanese Arts and Ways

道

From *chado*—"the Way of tea"—to *budo*—"the martial Way"—
Japan has succeeded in spiritualizing a number of classical arts.
The names of these skills often end in Do, also pronounced Michi,
meaning the "Way." By studying a Way in detail, we discover vital
principles that transcend the art and relate more broadly to the art
of living itself. Featuring the work of H. E. Davey and other select
authors, books in the series MICHI: JAPANESE ARTS AND WAYS
focus on these Do forms. They are about discipline and spirituality, about moving from the particular to the universal . . . to benefit
people of any culture.

Cho ni za shite michi o toi.
"Sitting in the morning and searching for the Way."
CHIEI

From tea ceremony to flower arrangement, every Do form ultimately amounts to an inquiry into the Way of the universe. The line is from Chiei's Sen-ji-mon. *Calligraphy by H. E. Davey.*

LIVING THE
JAPANESE
ARTS & WAYS

45 PATHS TO MEDITATION & BEAUTY

H. E. Davey

Foreword by Wayne Muromoto
Illustrations by Steve Aibel

Michi: Japanese Arts and Ways

Stone Bridge Press • Berkeley, California

Michi: Japanese Arts and Ways, volume 4. Series supervisor: H. E. Davey.

Published by Stone Bridge Press, P. O. Box 8208, Berkeley, CA 94707

TEL 510-524-8732 • sbp@stonebridge.com • www.stonebridge.com

Photography, artwork retouching, and icons by Steve Aibel.

All calligraphy and poetry translations by the author.

Cover design by Linda Ronan incorporating the character *michi*, meaning "Way."

Printed in the United States of America.

10 9 8 7 6 5 4 3 2 1   2008   2007   2006   2005   2004   2003

LIBRARY OF CONGRESS CATALOGING-IN-PUBLICATION DATA

Davey, H. E.
  Living the Japanese arts & ways: 45 paths to meditation & beauty /
  H. E. Davey.
      p. cm.—(Michi, Japanese arts and ways; v. 4)
  Includes bibliographical references.
  ISBN 1-880656-71-X
    1. Japan—Civilization. 2. Arts, Japanese. 3. Aesthetics, Japanese. 4.
  Meditation—Japan. I. Title: Living the Japanese arts and ways. II. Title. III. Series.
  DS821.D37 2003
  646.7—dc21
                                                    2002153843

CONTENTS

FOREWORD

I have thought long and hard about how to introduce readers to this book. All Japanese artistic Ways offer numerous benefits to the Western practitioner, and they utilize a wide variety of similar principles. Picking exactly which principles and benefits to discuss in this limited space wasn't easy, especially since I wanted to communicate the essence of all Japanese arts ranging from tea ceremony to martial arts. But then I remembered a story I like to tell.

It's about how I met my martial arts teacher, Ono Yotaro. Although this book isn't about martial arts, the story hints at something that goes beyond martial activities to include the essence of every Japanese art or Way. It begins after a rather hilarious martial arts demonstration in Ono Sensei's backyard training hall (largely at my expense). He'd invited me to join him over snacks and beer left from a party thrown for carpenters refinishing his house.

Ono Sensei and the rest of us students walked to his front yard in the dim moonlight. We sat on chairs and old stone grinding wheels strewn about his yard, which overlooked northern Kyoto, the ancient capital of Japan. It was only my third evening in Japan, and I was suffering from culture shock and jet lag.

Ono Sensei took out a bamboo flute and played the loveliest, loneliest melody on it, which stuck to my homesick heart. The song represented the forlorn calls of deer in the winter, seeking each other in the snow. Then he laughed and bade us to enjoy more food and drink as he grilled me about my personal background.

Upon discovering that I had studied Japanese literature in college, he said, "Do you understand *furyu?*"

I shook my head. "It's a literary concept used by the Heian courtiers of Kyoto . . . but I could never grasp what it meant. It was a very complex term."

"Not really," Ono Sensei said. "Furyu—wind and flowing waters. The literati loved life, but their lives were fleeting and often full of sorrow. Happiness can be as elusive as the wind or the waters of a river running through your hands. Furyu is what underlies our martial arts and all classical Japanese arts. It's a fleeting kind of beauty."

Ono Sensei continued. "Look, it sounds complicated, but it's really simple. The reason it's hard to explain logically is that it's a feeling, not a logical concept. Sitting here, in the dark with only candlelight, the stars and the city lights out there in the distance, talking with new and old friends, knowing that this moment will never come again . . . that is furyu. Simple as that."

Simple as that. And yet, like much of Japanese traditional culture, seeming simplicity hides a deepness and a complexity that takes decades to comprehend. In my case, after years of studying various Japanese arts, I still find myself learning anew the seemingly basic concepts and movements: how to hold a tea scoop properly, how to grasp an opponent's wrist, or how to pull a Japanese plane to shave off a hair-thin layer of wood. . . .

In this day and age, one is often asked what "good" is there in pursuing a particular pastime, as if everything in life has to be measured and quantified like a statistic. Yet even the Bible notes that there is no profit in gaining the entire world if one loses one's soul. There may be no direct worldly profit from pursuing the Do arts of Japan, but it gives us an opportunity to gain insight into our very soul.

H. E. Davey, an old friend and fellow traveler on the Way, has written a series of books pointing out the winding road that meanders up the Taoist Ways. In this book, he lays out the first steps. He is surely one of the few writers in the English language who is qualified to describe the general lay of this land. Davey Sensei has studied Japanese systems of calligraphy, yoga, healing arts, and classical martial arts for most of his life. He therefore goes beyond an academic, clinical survey of such arts, and also beyond a narrow, technique-oriented "how-to" type of book to give us the spiritual and conceptual foundations of the Do arts.

Finding such a teacher, who can verbalize such concepts, is a rarity even in Japan. This book will be of great service to people studying any of the Japanese arts, or anyone curious about what such study entails and offers the student.

Priests and warriors of old Japan once took to heart the study of these arts, placing mastery of seemingly effete and elitist disciplines like tea ceremony or flower arrangement on the same level as mastery of martial arts. So while a study of the Ways may not win you fame, fortune, or glory, it will offer you intangible benefits that those ancient people were all too cognizant of.

Tread lightly, dear reader, for such arts and their serious practitioners are rare. Finding a legitimate teacher takes some searching, but this book will be a wonderful start. If even a bit of the Way's true flavor can be tasted and passed on through you, then the dreams of our teachers will have been met: that their cherished Ways would be of service to us all, across cultures, across centuries, and across generations.

WAYNE MUROMOTO
Honolulu, Hawaii

WAYNE MUROMOTO, *a college instructor of journalism and graphic arts, grew up in the Japanese cultural arts. He graduated with a BA in Japanese literature and languages from Cornell University and holds an MFA in Fine Arts from the University of Hawaii. He publishes and edits* Furyu: The Budo Journal, *writes freelance, and has won several national poetry awards. He has studied traditional papermaking under Fujimori Yoichi Sensei in Japan, and he is an advanced practitioner of chado, the "Way of tea." He received comprehensive instruction at the Urasenke Foundation in Kyoto, where he lived and studied chado full-time. A longtime student and teacher of martial arts, he is a Shiban-Dai (Associate Professor) in the ancient Bitchu-den Takeuchi Ryu, which specializes in jujutsu grappling and weapons training. His permission to teach and issue rank was granted by Ono Yotaro Sensei, the Headmaster of this over-450-year-old art. Wayne Muromoto is the only American ever to receive this certification.*

PREFACE

Japanese arts and Ways have been growing in popularity around the world for decades. In the West, many people practice flower arrangement, bonsai, tea ceremony, shiatsu, and martial arts. Despite their wide popularity, however, Japanese arts (*geido*) are often misunderstood and distorted in the West. There is consequently a real need for literature that goes beyond the typical examination of the history and outward techniques of a single art form and that also exposes the lesser-known arts. What is most needed are comprehensive guides to what these arts are, where they came from, and how Westerners can successfully engage in them. Such guides are unfortunately rare. Writings that explore the more esoteric but immensely important aspects of these arts are rarer still. What are the underlying aesthetics of the Japanese arts? Some arts are touted as effective forms of "moving meditation," but how exactly do they function in this manner? What about the oft-mentioned but usually unexplained "spiritual dimensions" in the Japanese arts?

These esoteric aspects not only are inseparable from the technical and physical parts of practice, but they are also the elements of these arts that are most universal and applicable to the daily lives of non-Japanese practitioners. The lack of information about these universal principles masks the fact that, at their deepest levels, such arts as tea ceremony (*chado*), flower arrangement (*kado*), calligraphy (*shodo*), and martial arts (*budo*) are closely related. This book is intended to reveal, among others, this important aspect of these disciplines and to fill an important gap in the relevant literature.

Harmony of Mind and Body

Despite outward differences, Japanese arts share certain aesthetics; and more important, they demand the acquisition of related positive character traits for their successful performance. Notice that many of the names for these arts end in the Japanese word *Do*. Do means "the Way," and its use in these names indicates that an activity has surpassed its utilitarian purpose and been raised to the level of art, that its students are practicing it as a Way of life. In sum, a Do is an art that allows us to understand the ultimate nature of the whole of life by closely examining ourselves through a singular activity of life: to arrive at the universal through studying the particular.

Many artistic principles and mental states are universal to all Japanese Ways. One of the most meaningful and fundamental is the concept of mind and body coordination. Although few of us are required to use a calligraphy brush, Japanese sword, or tea ceremony utensils in daily life, learning how to use them skillfully can enhance our mental and physical health. Moreover, skill in these arts comes from integrating the mind and body. The important relationship between the mind and body and how to achieve mind-body harmony is also a principal theme of this book.

In Japanese calligraphy, teachers speak of a "unity of mind and brush" and declare that "if the mind is correct, the brush is correct." In Japanese swordsmanship (*kenjutsu*), it's usual to speak of a unity of mind, body, and sword. Mind and body coordination can be thought of as self-harmony. This integration is necessarily one of the mind and body in action, a central element for mastering any classical Japanese Way. But even if we aren't practicing a Japanese art or Way, we can all benefit from the principles of mind and body unification underlying the various Do.

It is absolutely true that practicing one of the Ways can lead to an understanding of the art of living life itself. Yet the teacher or book that can effectively demonstrate how the study of calligraphy or floral art can lead to spiritual understanding is rare; most simply pay lip service to showing the Way but fail to really offer clear explanations and effective techniques. It is commonly assumed that just throwing an opponent or manipulating a brush will somehow magically produce insight. Mere action will not lead to insight.

What to Expect from This Book

In fact, it's the manner in which we approach the Ways that determines what we learn from them. I've spent the majority of my life studying various Japanese arts, and speaking as someone who was once an excruciatingly shy, overweight, uncoordinated, and severely asthmatic child, I can confirm they offer a tremendous potential for self-transformation. The deliberate, conscious practice of Japanese Do forms *can* result in the cultivation of the mind and body. But they provide that potential; they don't guarantee it.

In order to fruitfully approach the tea ceremony, Japanese dance, or other arts as meditative acts, it's important to see exactly how they can lead to understanding. Many people arrange flowers, make tea, or practice the martial arts without any sudden insights into the nature of living taking place. I have attempted in this book to show principles and practices that will allow readers to directly experience these arts as meditation.

It's also important to keep in mind that cultural props like traditional dress and bowing are not inherently spiritual. Simply wearing a kimono or bowing does not express a meditative nature; it is the manner in which you bow, for example, and the invisible spirit of your practice that makes a Do a Way. This spirit and its importance is another topic addressed in this book.

Although all who write about the Japanese arts and Ways are themselves students of their disciplines, it's important to share the knowledge and insights one has gained for the benefit of others, and that has also motivated me to write this book. At the same time, while I want to share with readers my experiences and thoughts concerning the Ways, it would be a mistake if others view me as a spiritual authority or expert. I am not interested in an exalted status or celebrity.

To look to another for the truth is to bypass the Way of the universe that's right before our eyes. It is trying to see through the eyes of another and thus fated to result in delusion: the follower thinks she or he has seen the truth—whereas it is at best only a reflection of it—and the leader figures he or she must be doing something right because of the worshipful demeanor of the followers. The connection between such leaders and followers is, unfortunately, shared delusion. Still, many opt for following others, because looking for the truth invariably involves a leap into the unknown. And it's a leap we each must make by ourselves.

All of my books deal with meditation and spirituality in a Japanese context. Nevertheless, in these books I've tried to avoid telling readers *what to do*. Instead, I hope to offer readers a means to discover for themselves *how to do it*. It's not my place, or anyone else's for that matter, to tell you how to live, and although I write about spiritual and meditative arts, I'm not qualified to be anyone's "spiritual master." I doubt if anyone is so qualified. My aim in writing this book is simply to share meaningful techniques of mind and body coordination with others. I've learned a great deal in writing this work, and I hope my readers, too, will find the book a catalyst for their own growth.

Since many Japanese Ways involve physical activity to some extent, it's possible to sustain injury if you practice incorrectly or if you have a preexisting medical condition. It is important, therefore, to consult a medical professional before embarking on training of a physical nature. Practicing under the supervision of a qualified teacher is also advisable. As always, you are responsible for your own physical and psychological well-being.

How This Book Is Organized

To make this book easy to understand, I've arranged it logically. I start with the Chinese concept of *Tao* and explore how it became the Japanese Way; how, in other words, Japanese culture has interpreted the Chinese Tao. I also make a point of outlining exactly how the Ways of Japan function to lead us from the particular to the universal, and I discuss the nature of the Japanese Ways today.

In subsequent sections, I cover aesthetic principles found in the Japanese arts and give detailed information about their spiritual counterparts—ideas such as *ki* ("life energy"), *hara* ("abdominal centering"), *fudoshin* ("immovable mind"), and others. From this, you will discover how these artistic ideals and spiritual principles connect all of the Japanese art forms together. Whether you're interested in karate, tea ceremony, or flower arrangement, you'll find informative material that makes the study of these arts easier and illustrates how they're linked by a common set of little-understood principles. Better yet, you'll receive knowledge about these concepts that you might be able to positively incorporate into daily life.

To illustrate these aesthetic and spiritual principles, I take examples from a wide variety of Japanese arts and Ways, such as tea ceremony, flower arrangement, calligraphy, and others. They are merely representative examples, however. If I mention how a particular concept relates to the martial arts, for instance, the idea is rarely limited to that spe-

The glossary-style sidebars throughout this book present brief descriptions and definitions of Japanese Arts & Ways and words. The following icons are used at the ends of these to indicate what area of endeavor each belongs to:

Ideals of
the Way

Martial
Ways

Artistic
Ways

Performing
Arts

Traditional
Crafts

cific example and finds expression in other art forms as well. And though I may discuss how the substance of the Way expresses itself in the martial arts, that doesn't make this a martial arts book; the same can be said for examples taken from dance, Japanese gardening, and other classical arts.

Toward the end of the book, I discuss what to expect if you undertake the study of a classical Do. The number of people practicing flower arrangement, tea ceremony, ink painting, martial arts, and similar endeavors outside of Japan is vast. Unfortunately, so is the dropout rate. I could have included this section based simply on the great number of people who are studying, have studied, or are thinking about studying one of the Do. But when considering the relatively large turnover of Western students, I felt addressing how to study a Way and combat "culture shock" was something I needed to do here. These aspects have rarely been properly discussed in other books. I also include valuable information about what a traditional teacher will expect from you and how to successfully negotiate the hurdles faced by many newcomers to the Japanese Ways. An appendix includes important information about finding such a teacher.

Throughout the text are sidebars containing summaries of many of the traditional Japanese crafts, arts, and Ways mentioned in this volume or that you may run across in your further studies; these have been placed in alphabetical order, glossary-style, so that you can find them easily.

I occasionally cite Japanese poems and sayings for illustrative purposes. All translations are mine, some more literal than others.

Beauty is in the eye of the beholder and so is how we define Japanese aesthetics.

There isn't a universally agreed upon standard in Japan, and not everyone will concur with my explanations. Remember that this book's orientation is on the spiritual and meditative aspects of these concepts, which has influenced my interpretation of them.

You might enjoy my other books under the Michi: Japanese Arts & Ways imprint. *Brush Meditation: A Japanese Way to Mind & Body Harmony*, *The Japanese Way of the Flower: Ikebana as Moving Meditation*, and *Japanese Yoga: The Way of Dynamic Meditation* all discuss the nature of the Do—the Way of the universe. It's a Way I've been following since childhood. And although I miss the Way as often as I hit it, my writings aim at encouraging others to look directly at the actual nature of existence and see the Way that underlies all creation. I hope we can discover it together.

Acknowledgments

Although writing is ultimately a solitary activity, this book would not have been realized without the help of a number of people.

Peter Goodman, my publisher, editor, and friend, suggested this project to me not long after we first met. He seemed to think the book would be something I could write with authority. I appreciate his confidence in me, his friendship, and his support of my writing. The staff of Stone Bridge Press has also been a big help to me.

Ann Kameoka, my wife, has always supported not only my book projects but me as well. I'm very fortunate, and I'll always be grateful.

My late mother, Elaine, and my late father, Victor, both backed my lifelong involvement in the Japanese Ways. My dad, in fact, provided me with my first introduction to a traditional Japanese art. Our debt to our parents can never be repaid.

I'm also grateful to my friends Dave Lowry and Wayne Muromoto. Dave has written numerous books and articles about Japanese culture and martial arts. Several of his books gave me information that was useful in writing this work. Wayne publishes *Furyu* magazine and has written for the *Hawaii Herald*, a Japanese-American newspaper. I'm fortunate to have such knowledgeable friends who have given me fine feedback on my ideas and endured my long-distance phone monologues for years.

My students Terri Brown and Sean Souders posed for this book's illustrations. I appreciate their time and help. Sean started studying Japanese yoga and martial arts at my dojo when he was just four years old. He is now one of my best adult students.

Steve Aibel, another of my students, is an excellent artist. I'm grateful for his fine illustrations.

Finally, I couldn't have written this book without studying a variety of Japanese arts and Ways. In Shin-shin-toitsu-do (a system of Japanese yoga), budo, shodo, and other arts, I've had many outstanding teachers—too many to name in this limited space.

This book is dedicated to my *sempai* and *sensei* (seniors and teachers), both in the United States and Japan.

H. E. DAVEY
Green Valley, California

A NOTE ON THE JAPANESE LANGUAGE

Japanese is the international language of the Japanese arts and Ways, and even a modest knowledge of the Japanese language can open certain doors and lead to a deeper grasp of Japan's culture, thus making the practice of its cultural activities more meaningful. Knowledge of the language also allows the Western enthusiast to more easily interact with both Japanese experts and genuine Western authorities (many of whom have spent time training in Japan) without embarrassment. In fact, my knowledge of Japanese art terminology has proved to be a common bond between me and non-English-speaking artists from other Western countries. It's possible to read the Japanese words in this book and avoid embarrassment over mispronounced terms by following the guidelines below:

a is pronounced "ah" as in father
e is pronounced "eh" as in Edward
i is pronounced "ee" as in police
o is pronounced "oh" as in oats
u is pronounced "oo" as in tune

Doubled consonants (as in *kappa*, for example) are pronounced with a brief pause between syllables. The Japanese *r* is pronounced so that it sounds like something between English *r* and *l*. Further, Japanese doesn't have a plural form: thus *yubi* ("finger") can refer to one or more than one finger, depending on the context. The special orthographic signs called macrons, used in some books to indicate extended vowel sounds in Japanese, are not used here.

Last, according to traditional Japanese practice, it is customary to refer to a person by family name first and given name second. This custom has been followed throughout this volume. Sensei, a title of homage meaning "teacher," is always placed after an instructor's family name: Tanaka Sensei, for example.

THE 45 PATHS TO
MEDITATION & BEAUTY

Attributes of the Way

Harmony
Asymmetrical Balance
Artlessness
Impermanence
Unity with the Universe

See p. 78.

The Essence of the Japanese Arts & Ways

Spiritual Aesthetics in the Japanese Arts & Ways

Mind & Body Unification in the Japanese Arts & Ways

Traditions & Personal Relationships in the Japanese Arts & Ways

FURYU: *Furyu is composed of two characters: "wind" and "flowing." A renmentai shosho, or "connected cursive," script was used in this artwork to suggest flowing action. Like the moving wind, furyu can be sensed but not seen. It is both tangible and intangible in its suggested elegance. And like the wind, furyu points to a wordless ephemeral beauty that can only be experienced in the now, for in the next instant it will dissolve like the morning mist.*

Chapter 1

THE WAY

Japan's long history of importing, synthesizing, and recreating aspects of other cultures continues to this day. The primary source of such cultural borrowing in Japan's early history was China, whose civilization existed for centuries at a high level hardly seen in other parts of Asia. Chinese religions and spirituality had an immense impact on Japanese society and the Ways of Japan. Chinese religious development is marked by diversity and was heavily influenced by native as well as Indian beliefs. This diversity can be found in the multiform tradition known in the West as Taoism.

The Chinese Tao

> Something mysteriously formed,
> Born before heaven and earth,
> In the silence and the void,
> Standing alone and unchanging,
> Ever present and in motion.
> Perhaps it is the mother of ten thousand things.
> I do not know its name.
> Call it Tao.
> TAO TE CHING [1]

Taoism is based on the concept of the Tao. Most basically, Tao means "road" or "path"; in a spiritual context, it refers to "the Way." Taoism was (and is) grasped and

Aikido

The Way of union with the life energy (ki) of the universe, a modern martial Way founded by Ueshiba Morihei Sensei and derived from Daito Ryu aiki-jujutsu and other influences.

practiced in many forms, each reflecting the historical, societal, or individual circumstances of its disciples. This variety can be confusing, but some claim it explains the resiliency of Taoism. Its versatility has allowed it to evolve in accordance with the particular character of its followers.

Confucianism was the primary moral and ethical tradition in China. And, whereas Taoism has a relationship to Confucianism, it has avoided being absorbed by this major tradition, with which it has coexisted for generations. Taoism's persistence is remarkable in that Confucian traditions served as the moral and sacred bedrock of Chinese institutions, etiquette, and rites. Throughout Chinese history, people have tended to embrace both teachings, sometimes at different stages in life or according to individual disposition and preference. The phenomenon is not unlike the widespread embrace of both Shintoism and Buddhism in Japan. This long-standing phenomenon in China and Japan probably says as much about the Asian mindset as it does about Asian spirituality.

It is said that Taoist philosophy was established by Lao-tzu (literally "Old Master"), who is believed to have lived during the fifth century B.C. He is believed to be the compiler of the *Tao Te Ching*, or the *Classic of the Way and Its Power*. The sage Chuang-tzu, who lived in the third century B.C., contributed greatly to the evolution of Taoism through his philosophical tract known as *The Chuang-tzu*. The teachings of both men represent a reinterpretation and elaboration of an already rich Chinese heritage of beliefs based on veneration of nature and divination.

Both men lived during a period of cultural discord and religious unbelief. They advanced an idea of the Tao as being simultaneously the origin of all creation and the life power behind all action in nature. Both the Way and its power are beyond the limits of intellectual comprehension, but they can nevertheless be observed in the endless manifestations of nature. Within these natural manifestations and the Tao itself, Lao-tzu and Chuang-tzu saw evidence of a spiritual approach to being.

Further, owing to the social upheaval of the time, early Taoists envisioned Taoism as a means to establish a united and permanent secular order. The order in nature and the Tao was seen to be more reliable and timeless than the state and other societal fixtures and their underlying concepts created by humans. Thus, life could best be lived in agreement with the Tao, which, in essence, is a Way of living that is natural, simple, and free from all conditioning. The first Taoists taught that living prosperously was synonymous with harmonizing with the natural Way of the universe. This approach of noninterference and harmony was termed *wuwei*, "nonaction," or action that doesn't conflict with nature. In Japanese, this is called *mui*. It will be explored over the course of this book.

Confucian teachers were often seen in China as insightful, scholarly, and models of high moral character. Taoist *hsien*, or advanced mystics, were insightful in a related but radically different manner. (These advanced mystics were called *sen* or *sennin* in Japan; *sen* is the Japanese pronunciation of Chinese *hsien*.) Chuang-tzu wrote of savants who were, for example, craftsmen and woodworkers. Although humble in status, these artisans captured not merely the enigma of artistry but also the art of living. The Taoists viewed the artists' understanding of the essence of artistry and living well as arising from a concentrated mind, a mind existing in the moment, one that has transcended attachment to relative states and objectives such as wealth, fame, and power. The sages described in the *Tao Te Ching* and the *Chuang-tzu* embraced an art and a Way of life that accorded with the cycles of creation and destruction that pervade the absolute universe instead of merely following the transitory and relative values of society.

Although Chuang-tzu wrote of men who embraced the Tao

Aiki-jujutsu

"Jujutsu based on aiki." A martial art that's ultimately derived from the oshi-kiuchi combat techniques of the Aizu clan and popularized by Takeda Sokaku Sensei, disseminator of Daito Ryu aiki-jujutsu.

but remained in society, living with wives and children, it was common throughout Chinese antiquity for people tired of civilization and its trappings to withdraw from their social milieu and retreat to rural settings and join with the artless elegance of nature. Such seekers might create poetry about the cosmos or paint naturalistic scenes of splendor; Taoist breathing exercises and forms of meditation were practiced too—all were used to secure the life energy (*chi* in Chinese, *ki* in Japanese) that is inseparable from nature itself.

These sennin, variously described as "Taoist immortals," "sages," and "mystics," figure prominently in the Taoist universe, more so than is sometimes recognized. The Chinese character for *sen* is composed of a component representing "person" and one representing "mountain," indicating the Taoist inclination to retreat to the mountains in search of enlightenment.

> Religious Taoism stressed the idea of eremitism, which is implicit in the character for immortal, combining the characters for mountain and man. The rejection of the world of strife to live as a hermit is one aspect of the search for an ideal life of quietude. The quest for immortality and the pursuit of eremitism provided the abiding appeal of Taoism over the centuries.[2]

Mountains, owing perhaps to their lofty and awe-inspiring nature, occupy an important place also in the native Japanese Shinto religion. The sennin can be seen as equal parts man and myth, both aspects of which will be explored shortly.

Within China, a distinction between what might be called "original Taoism" and "popular Taoism" has never been clear. For our purposes, however, such a distinction is useful. Popular Taoism had (and has) a tendency to stress magic, fortune-telling, and related activities. Original (or perhaps "philosophical") Taoism, as explained in the *Tao Te Ching*, stresses universal harmony and natural action rather than magical rites for personal or material gain. Its concern is thus the human rather than the mystical component of the sennin. Popular Taoism, furthermore, gradually evolved a group of eight sennin, known in English as "the Eight Immortals," who were modeled after the Eighteen Arhats found in Buddhism. These eight sennin were advanced Taoist adepts who were believed to have attained immortality. This later claim of immortality was perhaps an attempt to successfully compete with the advancing influence of Indian Buddhism in China. In ancient Japan, some of the populace also embraced the lore of the Eight Immortals.

Taoist themes and art can be partly attributed to inspiring the Chinese love of nature and the tendency to abandon society in an attempt to gain enlightenment. They also encouraged a confirmation of life and health in the form of pursuits of vitality, long life, and even exemption from death. Lao-tzu reexamined and recast in a natural light the age-old deification of nature and the secret arts. Nevertheless, esoteric rites seeped back into Taoism as a desire to strengthen health and prolong life. Taoist alchemists searched for herbs and chemical compounds that could guarantee imperishability. Taoists sought the legendary mountain-dwelling sennin, who were regarded as either enlightened practitioners or actual immortals. In their pursuit of well-being and vigor, they explored herbal potions, developed principles of cooking and nutrition, and developed methods of exercise, healing, massage, breathing, and meditation to keep the mind and body youthful.

Said to be able to cure sickness, see into people's souls, and read the future, the sennin were viewed as mavericks, with their own set of values and way of life; yet, the stern moralistic retaliation of the Taoist gods actually fortified the conventional social mores. Thus, although Taoism was an alternative to Confucian-

Bonsai

Japanese dwarf trees, which vary from a few inches to several feet in height. Different approaches to cultivation exist, but they share common Japanese aesthetic qualities. Among these are simplicity, naturalness, harmony, and artlessness.

ism, it rarely endangered the established social structure. Some scholars suggest it was an important safety valve in the Chinese social order and a conduit for alternative ideas. Yet to an individual who clearly sees the actual nature of the Way—a nature that is primordial, universal, uncreated, and unconditioned by mere thoughts and beyond relative cultural values—the genuine Tao is much more than a social safety valve or system of magic whose end is the delusional elixir of immortality.

Considering ancient Japan's heavy borrowing from China's advanced culture—the Chinese system of writing and Buddhism are two prime examples—it was probably inevitable that Taoism and Taoist esoteric practices would be imported to Japan.

Tao into Do: Japanese Interpretation of the Way

Like many aspects of Chinese culture, Taoist shamans and concepts were eventually brought to old Japan. Taoist teachings, referred to in Japanese as Dokyo (do, meaning Tao, and kyo, "teachings") gradually influenced Japanese society and arts. Direct influence took place through interaction with Taoist adepts, while more indirect influences occurred via Chinese arts and practices shaped by Taoist principles, and through the wide introduction of Chinese Zen Buddhism, which also bore a Taoist influence.

> Do, of course, is the Japanese pronunciation of Tao, the metaphysical force of the ancient Chinese religion of Taoism, as much a ritual of alchemy as it was a philosophy that encouraged "going with the flow" of nature. Fused with Confucian concepts of etiquette, respect, and a devotion to tradition and learning, the seeds of the Tao were germinated in Japan, where they emerged not so much as

Budo

Martial ways; combat forms of personal growth derived from koryu bujutsu. See also koryu bujutsu.

a distinct religion but as ideals applied to the performance of native arts and crafts, evolving them into something much more.

The list of the Do forms in Japan is considerable. Occidentals are familiar with some that have been transplanted, more or less successfully, like judo and kado, or as it is better known, ikebana (flower arranging). But many others are virtually unheard of. There is kodo, for instance, the Way of incense appreciation, and togeido, the Way of pottery. Some are even more esoteric, such as shiseido, the Way of femininity.[3]

After Taoism was transplanted to Japan it quickly became "Japanized." The sennin lore of popular Taoism spread and was transformed in its new, fertile ground.

Gama was one of the mythical sennin embraced in certain sectors of Japanese society. He is usually depicted in Japanese art with a white, three-legged toad, whose form he could assume. Gama was also associated with Tekkai, who, like Gama, was said to be immortal. He was believed to be able to leave his body, an ability that on one unfortunate occasion had disastrous results: while his spirit was wandering about, his followers discovered his deathly body and burned it; Tekkai was then forced to occupy the body of a diseased beggar (perhaps a warning against unnatural practices!). Carrying an iron crutch, he was believed to help with the transmigration of souls.

Chokaro, another sennin, refused to serve the government in times of corruption. He is shown in art with a white mule that could carry him thousands of miles. Even better, Chokaro could fold his mule up like paper when it was no longer needed. Another sennin, Kinko, was a musician who rode on the back of a giant carp. One of the native Japanese sennin, Kume, could fly. These and other mythical Taoist adepts are depicted in many Japanese art forms, from painting to sculpture.

In China the label sennin (hsien) was applied not only to mythical personages but also to advanced Taoists. This distinction hasn't always been clear in Japan; nonetheless there have been in the past and still are today those who practice Taoist-oriented forms of spiritual cultivation. As Michio Kushi writes:

> Among these people, those principles led to the development of cosmically universal consciousness, along with health and longevity, and they were often called Sen-Nin, or "free men." There is much evidence including records, documents, and legendary stories about their unusual abilities.
>
> In the present there are still some people who train in this ancient macrobiotic way, Shin-Sen-Do, especially in the oriental countries—Japan, China, India, and others. Their existence, and these practices, are not widely known among modern civilized societies.[4]

Kushi, an ardent proponent of macrobiotics, refers to the Sen Do Ren, a group in Tokyo that studies Dokyo-based mind and body exercises known as Shin-Sen-Do (Shin: "gods" or "divine beings"; Sen, from sennin; and Do:"Way,"). Sen-do, Sen-jutsu, and Sennin-do are other designations used in arcane circles in contemporary Japan to indicate spiritual disciplines that trace their origins to esoteric Taoism. Associated healing arts are sometimes nonspecifically termed Sennin Ryoji, and though particular versions of these disciplines are fairly close to Chinese Taoist practices, many have widely diverged from their origins.

E. J. Harrison, a writer who lived in Japan in the early 1900s, detailed his impressions of Taoist influences in early twentieth-century Japan:

Bunka

Embroidery simulating a painting and using a punch needle. It was instituted about seventy years ago, when the punch-type needle came to Japan via Europe. After years of experimentation, the punch needle was fully developed and a four-ply rayon thread was perfected. Just two fundamental stitches are used in bunka: fluffy and straight. Variations of these stitches give bunka the look of a "painting by yarn."

. . . closer inquiry reveals the presence in society of a type of occult operator called by the Japanese Sennin—a word which I am inclined to render as "yogi" or "adept." While some of these yogi are known to pass their lives in the forests, or mountains, cut off as far as possible from communion with their kind, there are others who, although they have attained a high degree of occult development by persistent introspection, are yet content to pass the rest of their lives in the busy haunts of men and even pursuance of normal avocations.[5]

Many modern Japanese, however, know little of Dokyo and even less of Sennin-do (which is even misconstrued to relate to "1,000 people," based on the word for "thousand," *sen*, which, although pronounced the same, is represented with a different Chinese character). For this and other reasons, not all Taoist-inspired Ways in Japan directly acknowledge this debt in their names, histories, and literature. This is the case with, for example, the Shin-shin-toitsu-do system of Japanese yoga, which I practice and from which the mind-body exercises that will appear shortly are derived.

On the other hand, it is a mistake to think that every art whose name includes the designation Do has a deep or specifically Taoist origin. The Japanese Do has long since come to be used in a generic manner, and though it does have origins in the Chinese Tao and carries a similar meaning, in many Japanese arts, that is the extent of the connection. In any case, it's my belief that the Taoist connection is not always fully explored or acknowledged in writings about the Ways of Japan.

And what of Confucianism? Certainly along with Buddhism and a writing system, Confucianism was a cultural artifact the Japanese imported from China in a big way.

Bunraku

Bunraku, with Noh and Kabuki, is one of the three forms of traditional Japanese theater. It makes use of captivating puppets, each of which is animated by three black-clad puppeteers. The classical Bunraku repertoire often includes retellings of historical events as well as tragic love stories. A Bunraku troupe of puppeteers follows many traditional Japanese practices of the Way, such as strict training, observance of respect and hierarchy, and lifelong devotion to seamless execution of technique.

The Confucian Influence on the Japanese Ways

The impact of Confucianism—which continues to this day—on Japanese social mores, etiquette, government, and nearly all aspects of Japanese society was profound.

Historically, although the emperor usually reigned, he didn't always rule. For a significant portion of Japanese history, the shogun (military leader) and the *bakufu* (military government) held feudal Japan in an iron grip. Starting in 1603, after years of internal warfare, the bakufu of shogun Tokugawa Ieyasu ushered the country into a more peaceful era. The Edo period (1603–1867) was dominated by the autocratic Tokugawa family, whose bakufu made use of imported Confucian doctrines to provide ethical legitimacy to its administration. These doctrines still influence Japanese social strata, including the different Do. Confucianism, in its deep concern with societal behavior, has also affected the *reigi*, or formal etiquette, associated with a number of the Ways. (I discuss this in detail in chapter 4.)

The Tokugawas selected concepts from the conservative Chu Hsi style of Confucianism, ideas dealing with social decorum and filial piety, typically emphasized in Confucianism but also serving to bolster the Tokugawa view of a social order that ensured allegiance to the bakufu. Eventually, however, resentment of the Tokugawa brand of Confucianism (and the Tokugawa family itself) arose in several segments of society.

Bakufu administrators created a list of Confucian principles that were officially ratified by the government. These precepts were drawn from the teachings of Chu Hsi (1130–1200). His philosophy is known as Shu-shi or Tei-shu in Japanese. Its emphasis on loyalty to parents, social alliances, and duty to one's ruler made it an ideal means of promoting social cohesion and fidelity to the Tokugawa bakufu. In addition, however, the Neo-Confucianism of

Chu Hsi stressed investigating the universal by means of the particular, which is a central idea in all the Ways.

As dissatisfaction with the bakufu and its variety of Confucianism expanded in Japan, another form grew to rival Chu Hsi's doctrines. This new type was termed Oyomei in Japan and was based on the system of Wang Yang-ming (1472–1529). In opposition to the intellectual orientation of Chu Hsi, Oyomei stressed intuition and personal development. More important in relation to the evolution of the Do forms, Oyomei emphasized control of the mind through a process of systematic bodily disciplines such as what we now associate with the Ways. Wang advocated that virtue would result from such disciplines and felt that disciplined activity would give rise to a unity of thought and action, mind and body, an ideal that still lies at the very heart of the Japanese Do forms. He urged that action, more than words, was the way to self-perfection. Oyomei exhibits a simple and direct spirituality that has some similarities to Zen, but, unlike Zen, has seldom been credited in the West for its large role in shaping the Japanese arts and Ways.

Unfortunately for the Tokugawa bakufu, Oyomei also stressed individual worth over hereditary position. In any case, Oyomei Confucianism, closer to Taoism than orthodox Confucianism, clearly influenced the Do forms and had a historical impact on them as large as or larger than mainline Confucianism.

The Ways evolved and were influenced by both Confucianism and Taoism. But the Japanese seem to have been less inclined to think in metaphysical terms than the ancient Chinese, and their interpretation of the Do tends to be pragmatic and more concerned with social relationships. They were, in other words, as influenced by the Confucian Tao as they were by the Taoist Tao. Japan's societal conditions, feudal ruling class, and two influential religions—Shinto and Zen Buddhism—nonetheless modified both ideas.

Butoh

A present-day avant-garde Japanese dance form, initially performed in 1959. It blends dance, theater, improvisation, and Japanese established performing arts with German Expressionist dance and performance art.

Shinto and Zen Influences on the Japanese Ways

Chado

The Way of tea; also known as sado. The archetype of drinking powdered tea was brought to Japan from China in the twelfth century; chado was developed by Sen Rikyu in the sixteenth century. The tea used in chado comes from green tea leaves that are steamed, dried, and ground into a powder using a tea mill. Greatly influenced by Zen, chado emphasizes ideals of harmony, respect, purity, and tranquillity. A central teaching is ichi-go, ichi-e, "one encounter, one opportunity," which expresses the idea that a gathering for tea is a unique event that can never be repeated and so one should value every moment of it.

Zen and Shintoism have for centuries had a great impact on the entire Japanese cultural matrix, and both have likewise influenced the Ways. Shinto, which refers to the indigenous Japanese religion, means roughly "the Way of the gods." The term is thought perhaps to have originated in China, and indeed it can be found in ancient Taoist and Confucian writings. With no originator or original scriptures, Shinto centers on a reverence for all aspects of nature, including one's ancestors. Central to this concept is the idea that all parts of creation, animate and inanimate, have their own *kami*, perhaps best translated as "divine beings." The kami are believed to have protective capacities, and seeking their favor is a major part of the many Shinto festivals.

From Shinto, the Ways drew their traditional emphasis on purity and different purification practices (*misogi*). Purity is, in fact, one of the four maxims of the tea ceremony: harmony (*wa*), respect (*kei*), purity (*sei*), and peaceful solitude (*jaku*). Related to purity is the Shinto accent on cleanliness. Whether you visit a martial arts dojo or a school of calligraphy in Japan, it's common to see students engaged in *soji*, ritualistic cleaning of the training hall or practice room. Shintoism's focus on a reverence for nature has also formed an influence in the naturalistic emphasis of the Ways—in the form of practice, the style of the physical practice itself, and the aesthetics of the Do. *Sabi* ("rusticity") and *wabi* ("simplicity"), two fundamental elements in the aesthetics of the Ways, although also inspired by Zen, have profound Shinto overtones. These two elements are associated particularly with the tea ceremony, which, again, clearly shows influences from Zen.

The Zen Buddhist sect originated in India in the sixth century. Its originator is generally considered to be the monk Bodhidharma (Daruma in Japanese). Shortly after establishing Zen, in

about A.D. 520, he left for China, where, according to oral tradition, Daruma sat facing a wall for nine years until he attained
enlightenment.

The word "Zen" is the Japanese equivalent of Chinese
"Ch'an," which in turn comes from the Sanskrit Dhyana. The
monks Eisai (1141–1215) and Dogen (1200–53) introduced Zen
into Japan from China. Japan's martial ruling class promptly adopted it along with Shingon Buddhism, and with its message of deliv-
erance through meditation, it rapidly made inroads into most
aspects of Japanese existence. Zen's accent on being unobstructed
by intellectual questioning and realization of oneness with the universe affected all of Japanese culture, and many aesthetic qualities
have a historical relationship to Zen. Owing to its sweeping historical influence in Japan, Zen has touched most Japanese arts—
the tea ceremony, flower arrangement, and brush writing are a few
examples. Chado, or the Way of tea, one of the most important
Ways, has in particular had a long relationship with Zen and a
major impact on the other Ways.

Zen, in its link of meditation to daily activities, has made a
deep impression on the Japanese Do; indeed, the Ways have been
described as "plastic Zen." Zen stresses the avoidance of self-
deception, and the Ways have long served as a "reality check." It's
possible to imagine that we've achieved complete imperturbability
while sitting alone in meditation; yet, if this same Zen state cannot be demonstrated in Ways such as shodo or budo, real imperturbability has not been attained. If a student of shodo cannot
remain detached, even when his or her ink-laden brush is about to
cause a character to bleed, or if a kendo practitioner can't remain
calm in the face of a rapidly approaching bamboo sword, a Zen-
like imperturbability has not been genuinely realized. In Zen is
the idea that no matter how skillful our physical technique in tea
ceremony or the martial arts may appear, if the mind is not at

peace, the technique isn't representative of the Way. It is this Zen-related emphasis that allows the Ways to go beyond a particular activity and become arts that are capable of transforming all aspects of a person's life.

Although Zen is often mistakenly viewed in the West as the only body of spiritual teachings to significantly influence the Ways, a view that overlooks other important influences (like Esoteric Buddhism and Shingon Buddhism), it has indeed had a very deep and lasting impact. Perhaps the best source for a detailed discussion of Zen's relationship to the Do is the classic *Zen and the Ways*, by Trevor Leggett (see the notes and references at the end of this book). It covers the topic in far greater detail than is possible here and is recommended for interested readers.

Many Paths, a Single Way

Zen, Shinto, Confucianism, and Taoism all aided in the transformation of everyday Japanese arts and activities into viable spiritual paths. Nonetheless, an intellectual study of these religions will not result in an understanding of the Japanese Do forms; only actual participation will succeed. And when you deeply grasp one, you grasp them all.

To illustrate, when I began to study Japanese calligraphy and ink painting, I had already been involved in different Do since childhood. According to my teacher, Kobara Ranseki Sensei, I made unusually rapid progress. He regularly joked with me and the other students that I was a *meijin* ("genius"), but he once told me he really was baffled by my advancement. Eventually, when we were in Japan to show our work at the International Japanese Calligraphy Exhibition, I explained my background in other Do. I didn't want Sensei or my fellow students to believe that I thought I was "special" because I was a teacher of several Do. Only at this point, after a few years of studying shodo, did I feel comfortable explaining my previous training to him.

Kobara Sensei, acknowledged in Japan as one of the preeminent traditional calligraphers outside of Asia, nodded in recognition. Now, as he explained, he understood "my secret." As Kobara Sensei understood, and this is widely echoed in the Ways, if you genuinely grasp the essence of even one Do through firsthand experience, you have access to the sum and substance of all of them. This of course does not mean that a calligrapher will know the techniques of judo, for example, but it does mean that, on a very elemental plane, he or she will perceive the principles, aesthetics, and mental states common to all the Ways.

On another occasion, I heard my friend Shimbara Koyo Sensei, a high-ranking judo exponent, talking to a local student of Zen.

"What were you guys talkin' about?"

"Oh, we were just discussing the essence of Zen."

"I didn't know you were even interested in Zen."

"Well, I haven't read anything about its history, if that's what you mean . . . but I've practiced judo most of my life. We just figured out that we have a lot in common."

And what students of the Ways have in common is the Do itself, which isn't merely a particular way of doing a specific thing, but is actually the Way of the universe.

From the Particular to the Universal

Since all Japanese arts share the same aesthetics, the study of one Do can heighten the understanding of others. The same feeling of balance needed for skillfully "sculpting" a flower arrangement is needed in Japanese brush writing, in which every character

Do

The Way, a spiritual path (or michi), originally derived from the Chinese concept of the Tao. The names of many Japanese arts end in this designation, indicating their ultimate objective.

Do Chu no Sei

Do is "movement," while sei compares to "calmness." Do chu no sei describes "stillness in motion," or calmness in the midst (chu) of action. When Do forms, such as the martial arts or tea ceremony, are portrayed as forms of "moving meditation," it is this quality that is being expressed. Many Ways involve activity, often in relationship to others. They are usually performed with the eyes open, and as a result, when practiced as dynamic meditation, they relate closely to life. They can also help us translate seated meditation into activity.

exhibits a dynamic balance. In *odori*, or Japanese classical dance, and the martial arts, participants likewise master a dynamic balance that is analogous to the balance aimed at in Japanese calligraphy.

The identical unity with nature stressed in flower arrangement is also accentuated in martial ways like aikido and *aiki-jujutsu*, while shodo demands an intense attention to detail and brush form that is not incompatible with the methodical exactitude cultivated by disciples of ikebana. *Cha-no-yu*, or the "tea ceremony," is based on wa-kei-sei-jaku ("harmony-respect-purity-solitude"), and both Japanese calligraphy and flower arrangement seek to manifest related capabilities. Wabi and sabi are specific expressions of the philosophical foundation of the tea ceremony, and they are also artistic, even spiritual, attributes universal to all the Japanese arts.

In short, a thorough study of a particular Way allows us to assimilate these qualities and apply them to the practice of unlike art forms. The opposite is also true: many Western students of miscellaneous Japanese cultural arts commonly miss out on the consequence of these ideas, and in the end practice a pale imitation of the authentic art that they are studying.

Japan has traditionally excelled in "spiritualizing" activities like brush writing, dance, drama, and flower arranging. The ultimate goal in these Do is to see the whole of life through a particular practice or individual part of living. Master calligrapher, Zen expert, and founder of Muto Ryu swordsmanship, Yamaoka Tesshu, said that one of his principal teachings was "the practice of unifying particulars and universals." D. T. Suzuki, author of many books on Zen, in like manner referred to "the One in the Many and the Many in the One."

A certain procedure or copying exercise, for example, can be considered as a "particular." In *sumi-e*, ink painting, the aim in copying the teacher's rendering of a branch of bamboo is not to make merely a flawless duplicate; rather, the goal is to discover the essential quality, contained inside a given lesson or particular technique, of all techniques. We copy and study a particular model to lay hold of the universal principles that allow the technique to operate in the first place and that will at last empower us to rise above form to discover the formless. In so doing, it is often possible to perceive that these universal principles comprise something much greater than the singular art we're studying, that they amount to indispensable lessons in living.

On a more penetrating level, ikebana experts speak of achieving a state where they discern the actual characteristics of the blossoms they'll be arranging. They merge with nature, so that the particular (the arranger) unites with the universal (nature). Martial artists also speak of becoming one with their opponent and even the universe itself. The ultimate aesthetic running through every Japanese Way is a naturalness in which the difference between the individual and the universe softens into oneness.

The Japanese Ways Today

There are many Japanese arts and Ways, and while it's beyond the scope of this book to explore all of them or offer complete descriptions of the ones chosen for brief depiction, it is important in a volume of this sort to offer an overview of prevalent Japanese arts, crafts, and Ways.

What's more, although all of the Ways can be thought of as art forms, not all Japanese cultural arts are inevitably being practiced as Ways. Deplorably, not all bona fide Do forms, especially in Western countries, but also in modern Japan, are really being studied as Ways. Their proponents have often allowed the program of instruction in these Do to become purely physical and/or superficial in nature.

MUI: *"Do nothing."* Mui *is painted in the cursive and abstract sosho style of Kobara Ranseki Sensei.*
It refers to a state in which nothing is forced, contrived, or out of harmony with nature.

Chapter 2

AESTHETICS OF
THE WAY

Certain philosophical and aesthetic standards are shared by all Japanese arts. From the martial arts, to Japanese dance, to flower arrangement, distinctive artistic codes are held in common. These aesthetic codes have had a profound effect on the unfolding of the Ways. If they are not absorbed, no great appreciation of any Japanese cultural art is likely.

The large body of terms and theories allied with the aesthetics of Japanese art is beyond the reach of this book, and indeed, legitimate mastery of these principles comes only through individual, hands-on experience. But I would be remiss if I didn't note here at least the more significant of them. All of these principles connect to one another to form the harmonious totality of the Japanese arts and Ways. The descriptions of some terms and concepts thus sound similar: they are simply different methods of describing aspects of a singular entity—the Way.

The following list of attributes, which will be elaborated upon at the end of this chapter, represents a summary of my understanding of the aesthetics of the Way:

- Harmony
- Asymmetrical balance
- Artlessness
- Impermanence
- Unity with the universe

Some observers of Japan have noted that it is a culture of contradictions, and the same can be said for the aesthetics of the Japanese arts and Ways. Noh drama, for example, mirrors the Japanese affection for artlessness, understatement, subtle expression, and representative motions. But Kabuki drama employs larger-than-life mannerisms, passionate oration, and dazzling stage effects. Consequently, like any generalizations, these five attributes are not invariably applicable, but they do offer a beginning point for examining Japanese aesthetics. And I hope, as you read through this chapter, you will discover that the Way lies in embracing and transcending duality, thus entering a state in which all contradictions dissolve.

With these attributes in mind, then, let's examine the most important principles underlying the Japanese arts and Ways.

Wabi

In the West, or the United States at least, it is difficult to pinpoint a universally accepted definition of beauty. I exaggerate only a little when I say this isn't the case in Japan. In Western countries few people pay serious attention to aesthetics, aside from professionals working in artistic circles. True, an interior decorator may have a specialist's sense of what looks good in your house, but this rarely extends to your garden or your car. And we look for a car that appeals to whatever sense of style we subscribe to, but few long-lasting, overriding aesthetic principles guide this type of purchase. The generic, four-in-a-box, everyman appeal of the typical economy car isn't mirrored in the metallic insect on wheels, newfangled hot rod look of the Plymouth Prowler—automobiles that both have their fans. We can say the same for our taste in houses, furniture, and other items.

In Japan, however, most classical arts and Ways have shared common aesthetics for generations. Through the practice of nearly ubiquitous disciplines, the Japanese populace has been exposed to an almost universally acknowledged set of aesthetics. Although these aesthetics are frequently missing in the urban concrete sprawl of cities like Tokyo, nonetheless, in backdoor bonsai, a cherished antique in the home, the design of traditional clothing, and countless other forms, the Japanese is aware of a commonly affirmed aesthetic. Not only is there a common awareness but also there is widespread participation among Japanese in arts devoted to classical concepts of elegance and beauty.

Ride a train any evening in Japan, and you'll see it filled with women in kimono coming from tea ceremony class, students carrying kendo swords and armor, elderly people with samisen instruments—the list is long. At times I've wondered if every person in Japan is studying, or has studied, some traditional art form, and my experience is that in fact most people have or are doing so.

Owing to this widespread proliferation of traditional arts and Ways, the Japanese have come to embrace universal aesthetics, or *bigaku*, that first arose around A.D. 700 in the rarefied lives of the Japanese priesthood and royalty. These aesthetics soon filtered down into the everyday lives of ordinary people, and into the Do forms. They affect everything in Japan, from the way a house is decorated, to its outdoor garden, to the color of the car in the garage.

True, Japan has embraced Western artistic ideas, but they have often been modified by the Japanese sense of beauty. And of course not every Japanese thinks about such matters in the same way, or at all, but most have a clearer idea (but not necessarily a deep understanding) of what their traditional aesthetics are than is found in the West. One of the most important artistic sensibilities in Japan is wabi. Wabi is one of several key terms in the vocabulary of Japanese aesthetics. This vocabulary is called *fuzei* and refers to words that describe particular artistic feelings, sensibilities, and ways of seeing. Wabi is also a term that strongly resists easy definition.

Fudoshin

"An immovable mind." A state of mind that remains peaceful and undisturbed. Its physical expression is a posture so stable that it may seem immovable as well—fudotai, the "unmoving body." See also fudotai.

In wabi art, we find elegance with a feeling of austerity. Wabi is the recognition that beauty can be found even in the depths of poverty, and that beauty isn't limited to expensive, formal works of art produced by recognized masters. In fact, objects of great elegance can be constructed out of simple, inexpensive components. (It is interesting to note that tea ceremony utensils, which originally exhibited a rustic wabi style, can be extremely expensive nowadays.) A traditional Japanese wooden house is an example of the unpolished appeal of wabi.

On the other hand, Sen no Rikyu, who promoted wabi-style tea ceremony, once remarked that a tea caddy, owned by an acquaintance and made by a famed craftsman, was lacking in the spirit of wabi. The caddy was later broken into pieces and skillfully repaired. Upon a subsequent visit to his friend's house, Rikyu spied the restored caddy and promptly declared it a work now imbued with wabi.

In the Japanese arts and Ways, simple and natural don't necessarily equate to quick and easy. In calligraphy, for example, although a work might look like it was dashed off in a frenzy of artistic inspiration—characters about to leap off the paper—it was likely the result of hundreds of dry runs and failed experiments. And even if it was brushed in only a few moments, the skill that allowed art to be produced in a brief time was the result of years of training.

Simplicity can be achieved when skill is present, but being able to consistently hit this "sweet spot" can take years of experience. In shodo, the character for *ichi* ("one"), which consists of nothing but a single horizontal line, is considered to be among the most difficult characters to paint effectively. Likewise, when a martial arts teacher downs an opponent with just a small step forward and a slight motion of the arm, you're seeing budo at a high level. Defeating an attacker with many movements and an exaggerated display of technique is actually the crudest approach to combat, while ending the encounter with just a single glance, before any physical action takes place, is one of the ultimate goals of the Japanese martial Ways. Such simplicity has great depth, and it is inspired in the martial arts, shodo, flower arrangement, and other Do by consciousness of wabi.

The literal meaning of wabi is "poverty," but in aesthetics what is understood is a poverty of superficiality and artificiality. Wabi lies in finding that intangible, but valuable, "something" within ourselves and our art that defies trends and is timeless. To find value on the inside and in the soul of things, rather than in their monetary worth—or in monetary worth itself—is to cleave to the spirit of wabi. There is a Zen saying:

> *Ware tada taru o shiru.*
> I don't know much. I only know that I'm perfectly satisfied.

This expresses the essence of the wabi attitude of acceptance, in which being at peace in nature is valued above luxury, wealth, and opulence.

Once this understanding of our innate nature, as well as our innate unity with nature itself, is firmly recognized, then every moment and aspect of our lives is transformed. Whether at home, outdoors, in the city, or in the country, our lives can reflect an essential naturalness, simplicity, and ease of living that are our birthright. This is *wabi-zumai*, or "a wabi lifestyle," and it goes beyond a mere preference for an uncomplicated, unaffected, natural mode of living. Wabi-zumai is as much about *what we are* as it is about where we are, what we wear, and other externals. This natural Way of being, along with the principles of mental and physical harmony that can lead to it, will be discussed in chapter 3.

Fudotai

"Unmoving body." Refers to a stable posture that appears unmovable and is the physical expression of fudoshin. See also fudoshin.

Sabi

As I look about,
The flowers and maple leaves
Have long since vanished—
Just thatched roofed huts by the sea . . .
Merging with autumn twilight.

Hundreds of years ago, the poet Fujiwara Sadaie composed this ode to a singular austere moment . . . a moment that was gone before his ink-laden brush touched paper, and a moment that is still echoing through endless time. In this *waka* poem (Figure 1), both the view and the viewer have merged into a solitary unit. Fujiwara hints at an ageless sliver of eternity, in which the individual and the universal melt into a sole, absolute one that's resting motionless and unconditionally alone. Encompassing everything and thus nothing, endlessly fluctuating and therefore unchanging, swallowing up all creations and containing all things to form the absolute one that dissolves duality: it is the totality of existence.

By its very nature, it is utterly alone. A singularity containing every speck of time and space within infinite borders, it is unaccompanied but never lonely. Fujiwara sensed, and then portrayed, solitariness and detachment, but without a trace of lonesomeness, a condition totally autonomous and yet still linked to all things . . . but not clinging to them. It is a feeling of embracing while letting go. In the Do, this is called sabi, and it allows life to disappear back into itself without remorse or longing.

D. T. Suzuki was one of the first writers to explore in English the spiritual complexities of two elementally simple concepts— wabi and sabi:

Just to be tranquil or passive is not *sabi* nor is it *wabi*.

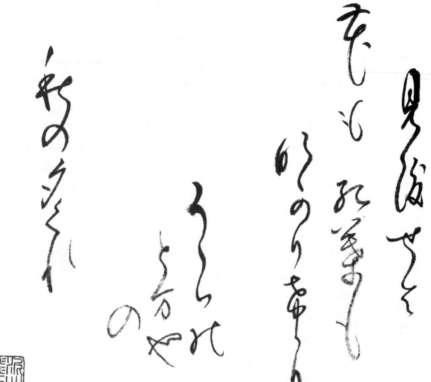

There is always something objective that evokes a mood to be called *wabi*. And *wabi* is not merely a psychological reaction to a certain pattern of environment. There is an active principle of aestheticism in it; when this is lacking poverty becomes indigence, aloneness becomes ostracism or misanthropy or inhuman unsociability. *Wabi* or *sabi*, therefore, may be defined as an active aesthetical appreciation of poverty. . . . Nowadays, as these terms are used, we may say that *sabi* applies more to the individual objects [of the tea ceremony, for example] and environment generally, and *wabi* to the living of a life ordinarily associated with poverty or insufficiency or imperfection. *Sabi* is thus more objective, whereas *wabi* is more subjective and personal.[6]

FIG. 1.
Miwataseba / hana mo momiji mo / nakarikeri / ura no tomaya no / aki no yugure.

"As I look about, / the flowers and maple leaves / have long since vanished— / just thatched roofed huts by the sea . . . / merging with autumn twilight."
FUJIWARA SADAIE

45

Funi

Non-duality, where the Creator and the created can be distinguished from one another but ultimately cannot be divided. Funi hints at the true nature of existence, which transcends cultural and relative distinctions. It points at a state in which the separation between us and others, between life and death, dissolves. And with the dissolving of duality comes the transcendence of fear as well as conflict of every kind. The Ways offer a means of experimenting with the nature of funi.

We shouldn't, however, take these comments in too literal a manner. Sabi can also make reference to a spiritual quality and a psychological state. It isn't used exclusively to describe individual objects. Plus, not all Japanese practitioners of the arts and Ways use the terms here in exactly the same manner. In short, no universally accepted and precisely delineated definition of wabi and sabi exists in Japan. And Rikyu, perhaps history's most famous advocate of the wabi-sabi aesthetic in chado, wasn't a poor man who lived far from his kind, alone in a hut—far from it. While wabi and sabi can be lived out literally, they point to the spirit of living in a certain mode, with a particular sensibility, as much as to the specifics of location, house, or occupation.

Along these lines, we can say that in Japanese art circles, wabi tends to refer more to our lifestyle (wabi-zumai), while we might describe an elegantly simple vase as having a "sabi feeling to it." Nonetheless, the aesthetic sense evoked by both wabi and sabi suggests that the terms are interrelated, although the distinction and usage pointed to above are typical among Japanese artisans devoted to the essence of wabi-sabi.

Sabi, like wabi, contains simplicity and austerity in its aesthetic makeup, and the two terms can be used together, so that it's possible to speak of something as having a wabi-sabi feeling to it. Nevertheless, sabi has its unique implications, such as the sense of solitariness mentioned above. In chado, sabi makes up one of four basic principles, in which case it is pronounced *jaku*. (The others, mentioned previously, are wa, "harmony," kei, "respect," and sei, "purity.") Jaku implies peacefulness, and this is also a central aspect of the sabi sensibility. In this sense, sabi refers to a spiritually independent state, a condition that is connected to all things while being absolutely alone and unaffected by the myriad creations of the world. This solitariness is called *sabi-shiori*. Such a state of timeless, solitary serenity lies at the core of sabi.

The aesthetic of sabi is also one of melancholy, summoned by, for example, verdigris and patina. It is the antique, rustic appearance of things after lengthy and loving handling—but before old age fully consumes them. In Japan, such a patina is often appreciated since it indicates that a work of art has passed through many hands, an extended succession of human hands. Blemishes and age spots give the object a humanistic property, a certain personality, and consequently make it more aesthetically inviting.

In the West, our enchantment with science and industrialization have made us fans of the modern and the automated. Our tendency has been, therefore, to miss the beautiful patina of age or to avoid objects that appear imperfect. Asia, in contrast, was less overwhelmed by either the scientific advancement succeeding the Renaissance in Europe or the engineering progress following the Industrial Revolution in the Western world. Following the Renaissance, Western art grew apart from its traditional link to human enterprise. In Japan, however, art and existence remained more integrated. Westerners have been inclined to concentrate on the sciences and commerce, leaving the practice of art to individuals designated as artists. The Japanese, on the other hand, have had a greater inclination to remain close to the arts and directly involved in them. Because art in Japan was more integrated into daily life, slight differentiation was made between the beautiful and the usable, an idea that ties into the sabi aesthetic. As expressed in this aesthetic, even everyday things became both elegant and practical.

Certainly the preceding observations are general, and exceptions can be found in both the East and West. And they pertain to a traditional orientation that is, however, being rapidly altered. From the late nineteenth century, the East and West began a period of mutual influence that continues today. Nonetheless, the gen-

Furabo

Related to fuga and furyu, indicates a person who roams about, unattached, carried like a slender piece of cloth fluttering in the wind. See also fuga; furyu.

eralizations about Japan point to a context in which aesthetics such as wabi and sabi evolved.

Sabi beckons to us in objects that evoke the resonance and unevenness that time bestows. In the classical Japanese garden (*niwa*), certain areas may at first appear as if nature has taken over, but if we look more closely, we see how human creativity has actually merged with nature to give birth to a sabi effect. Sabi is best expressed by the use of natural objects. In the garden, much use is made of bamboo (for fences, for example), rocks, straw, tree bark, moss, and the like. All of these things are incorporated into the design of the garden so that as they age and settle into the landscape they will express sabi. Gradually these things are altered by their inescapable advance toward dissolution, and this too is incorporated into the niwa, hence the melancholy appeal of sabi.

Rustic objects, autumn and winter, sunsets and twilight, the willing embrace of solitariness, like an evening spent trapped alone in a cabin in the backwoods by a sudden cloudburst, welcoming the charged stillness—all express sabi, which in turn expresses a self-governing beauty. It is an elegance that is consummated not just by human beings but by the universe through its natural course.

Mono no Aware

Mono no aware has been said to describe a sentiment of pathos relating to the fleeting nature of our relative world. In addition to a feeling of life's fragility, mono no aware relates to seeing beauty in this fragile, impermanent nature, and even grasping that without impermanence, genuine beauty cannot exist.

Nothingness is permanent, and everything is momentary. Accompanying this recognition is a moment outside of time, a moment that lasts throughout eternity, a moment that passes before we can absorb the words I've just written.

Experiencing the fragility of life affirms the worth of living. Beauty fades as quickly as it is experienced and thus it lives forever. And the moment passes so instantaneously that it cannot be contained by the intellect, making it everlasting. Mono no aware embraces all of these assertions.

These aspects might appear opposed—as in fact they are—but they are not contradictory. Let's look at them one by one.

First, though we might wish to believe otherwise, all living things are vulnerable to dissolution. Whereas the life force continues, the relative, changing aspects of us—our physical selves—are impermanent. This of course applies to all objects of creation. And it is the beauty of things, the beauty in their fleeting nature, and the evanescence of beauty too that are evoked by mono no aware.

When we see a dancer unexpectedly leap into the air with incredible grace, the beauty of the action captures the mind in an instant—and in the next instant it's gone. We glimpse the elegant movement of tall trees curtsying in the wind, but this too lasts only a moment. This sudden awareness of a fleeting beauty is well illustrated by a shooting star. Even a painting, which we can look at over and over again, often has its greatest impact when our gaze is first frozen by its magnitude. While we might look at it many times after, the real impression of beauty in its fullest force occurs only once—unless we grasp the art of seeing.

To wholly see beauty (or any aspect of living), the mind must be in the moment. Physical existence is now, with the past and future functioning as ideas rather than actual reality. Experience of beauty, and of life more generally, does not happen in the future, which is an imagined time that might not ever take place, or in the past, which no longer exists. The full experiencing of life and art must be now or not at all.

Furyu

From two words meaning, "wind" and "flowing." It suggests an elegance both tangible and intangible, an inexpressible, ephemeral beauty that can be experienced only in the moment, for in the next instant it will dissolve like the morning mist. See also fuga; furabo.

Yet the mind clings to the known, to the past, out of a striving for security. We eat a wonderful dinner or see a fantastic sunset, and the mind seeks to hold onto and sustain the wonder, awe, and happiness. Unfortunately, a mind that's caught in the past, that compares now to before, rarely experiences the present in a full way. By constantly comparing what we sense now versus what we once felt, we deaden all of our present experiences. The beauty expessed by mono no aware is a beauty of only this instant.

Like the past, which is only a memory, the future is an idea, not reality. The now, however, genuinely exists. This instant is real, but it is fleeting. And experience of the present instant cannot be used to predict the next instant. Just because we have started each day with a shower for the past twenty years, we have no contract with the universe that assures us the hot water will be working tomorrow.

Like the sense of security that stems from clinging to the past, "knowing" is an illusion. Reality lies in the unknown. If we realize and embrace this fact we discover that the only security in life comes from accepting and adapting to the instant, to a moment that is brief and transitory. To embrace change and the unknown is in the spirit of mono no aware. Mono no aware relates to harmony with the constantly changing universe and with universal cycles of creation and destruction.

A mind that resides in the instant can encounter beauty in its greatest breadth, from instant to instant. Although the beauty of a painting is often completely experienced only upon first sight, this need not be the case. If the mind abides in the moment, and then lets that instant die, and rests fully in a new instant, that beauty can again be fully appreciated. We can encounter a work of art, a food, or a natural landscape many times without diminishing its splendor. To understand mono no aware, we need to grasp that beauty and life exist in the instant. In mono no aware, we let the past dissolve, realizing that destruction is ultimately a positive act of creation. This realization manifests in a number of ways in the Japanese Do forms.

Shoshin

Shoshin means "beginner's mind," and it is believed to derive from Zen. It isn't so much an aesthetic concept as it is a state of mind. Nonetheless, this mental condition is needed to understand mono no aware and other aesthetics, which is why it is included in this chapter.

Shoshin describes a consciousness that's always fresh, never bogged down by its own past. In the condition of shoshin, we look at each lesson or practice session in a given art as if it were our first time to experience it, and this should be true even in the case of techniques and exercises that have been practiced thousands of times. With the shoshin mindset, we can continue to learn year after year, never reaching the point where we think we've learned all there is to know about a certain art or facet of that art. Thus, we assure a never-ending growth and development in an art that never grows tiresome.

Still, shoshin goes deeper than avoiding the complacent assumption that all there is to know has already been learned. Authentic shoshin is encountered in a mind that doesn't cling to the past and experiences the present wholeheartedly. It's this mind that retains a bona fide beginner's attitude, recognizing that past training is no guarantee of present success or even of an appropriate understanding. Every instant is ultimately different, and art, beauty, and success must be found right in that instant or it will not take place.

Let's look at an example. Shodo calligraphy students spend

Gagaku

One of the ancient forms of Japanese music. In 701, the Imperial Court Office of Music was created. Gagaku, "imperial court music," was the result. It is still performed under the direction of the Imperial Household Agency.

Go

An ancient game played on a square board divided into 361 squares. Two players take turns placing small, round, black or white stones on the board. The objective is to enclose as much area as possible. The person who surrounds the biggest section wins. Go is valued as a means of enhancing concentration and learning strategies that some claim are applicable to daily living. As in the modern martial Ways, players of go are promoted through a series of ranks.

many hours each week copying from *tehon*, which are models of characters brushed by advanced artists. Over the years that I've studied shodo, I've heard many novices remark that, even after making dozens of copies of the tehon, the first copies are the best; the more they practice, the worse they do. Is there something killing the realization of skill? Indeed there is.

As I noted, it's not uncommon for beginners to complain that practice results in a lessening of quality, and the natural question is why—why would more practice cause worse skill? Part of the answer lies in the mind's tendency to intrude the past into the present.

When we first copy a work of art, it's new. Our reactions to what we're attempting to reproduce are also new, and so are our successes and problems with the particular tehon. But as we continue to copy, layer upon layer of the past piles onto the current moment, making an accurate perception of what we're really looking at, and what we're actually doing, difficult. Soon, we're no longer looking at the piece we're trying to faithfully copy, but rather we're seeing only *our own representation of reality*. This representation contains all of our impressions, beliefs, prejudices, fears, desires, etc., that relate to the observed object and our effort to skillfully copy it. The more experiences we have with the object and the act of attempting to copy it, the more we tend to filter what we see through this veil of conditioning.

For instance, making a straight line in shodo or ink painting can be difficult. The line often wavers. This isn't necessarily a problem, as with practice most people can make a fairly even line. The mechanics aren't that complicated, but the mind can certainly complicate matters, and this typically takes place when we initially meet with failure. Then, if the mind clings to this failure, each time we try to create a straight line, we see that line through the veil of past failures. Since the mind controls the body, when we retain images of past wavering lines, our present line also wobbles. In short, we "psych ourselves out."

Avoiding this common tendency requires nonattachment, a state in which we live through each moment completely and let it dissolve, rather than clinging to it. And a mind that isn't in the moment inherently clings to the past. By practicing Japanese arts and Ways, we can discover a mind that rests in the instant, in a moment that is timeless. In this condition, each time we see a tehon to be copied, a sunset, or even our own house, the experience is fresh and new. We see *what is* instead of *our representation of what is.*

Donald Richie, a longtime resident of Japan and observer of its culture, makes the following observation about this nonattachment:

> By sacrificing an urge to immortality, and through a knowing acceptance of himself and his world, he [the Japanese] stops time. He has found a way to freeze it, to suspend it, to make it permanent. He does this, not through pyramids and ziggurats, but by letting it have its own way.[7]

Richie points to the timeless permanence in constant change that is revealed in the traditional Japanese garden. In the niwa, flowers bloom in the spring and leaves flutter to the ground in autumn, but the rocks, water, and essential landscape—the garden's structure—are invariable.

> The Japanese garden is like a still picture—a frozen moment which is also all eternity. It remains the same no matter the season because the seasons are acknowledged, and this acknowledgment is spiritual, a combination of idea and emotion.[8]

The present is outside of time. No matter how quickly we say that we're aware of the present, the moment has already past. It can't be clung to or measured. Thus, a full experience of beauty, indeed of all things, is possible only in the moment, and since the moment cannot be contained or clung to, beauty is found in an instant that is dissolving.

Clinging to moments that have passed precludes knowing the newness of each moment. The aesthetics of mono no aware and shoshin reveal the understanding that reality exists in an instant beyond time . . . and so it lasts forever. Beauty is indeed beautiful and fresh precisely because it is always new, spontaneous, and in the moment. It's special because it can't be preserved or recreated. With this comprehension comes the ability to see beauty in every fragile facet of life, even in the fading of a flower or the aging of a friend.

In this way, shoshin, mono no aware, wabi, and sabi are related. Shoshin is a beginner's mind that sees each moment in life as the first and only time that moment can be experienced. Mono no aware is an awareness of the fleeting and fragile nature of life, the fact that all created things deteriorate and dissolve back into the universe. Wabi-sabi correlates to an appreciation of this gradual dissolution, finding beauty in the rustic patina of age. In a material sense, the wabi-sabi aesthetic finds elegance in such a patina, while mono no aware recognizes that this patina is the result of inevitable natural corrosion, and even deterioration can be beautiful to a mind that doesn't compare the present to the past, the new to the old. This mind recognizes mono no aware rests in the present and perceives the indivisibility in birth-death, creation-destruction, and duality itself. It grasps a beauty that is absolute, that has no opposite, that contains no conflict between the inevitable and the wished for.

The element common to these principles speaks ultimately

to an acceptance of ourselves. For to accept ourselves completely, we must also embrace our own mortality.

Furyu

Furyu is composed of two elements: "wind" and "flowing." Like the wind, it can be sensed but not seen. It is a quality both tangible and intangible in its suggested elegance. Furyu points to an ephemeral beauty that can only be experienced in the now, for in the next instant it will dissolve like the morning mist.

> An ancient pond
> A frog leaps—
> The sound of water.

Basho's most famous haiku, in fact *the* most famous haiku (Figure 2), describes a moment of furyu that is at once simple and yet easily missed by those lacking in the furyu spirit. Think of it as a poetic snapshot, a split second in nature in which time ends.

Basho taught that the spirit of haiku is the spirit of *fuga*. Fuga means, "refinement of living." Yet this refinement isn't merely a matter of education, breeding, and financial stability, as is often assumed in modern times. Basho's fuga stemmed from the wabi-sabi philosophy of old Japan, and it correlates to a profound appreciation of and closeness to nature. Basho described it as being "a companion of the four seasons" in his *Yoshino Journal*. He further described his fellow poets, who were imbued with the character of fuga, as *furabo*—people who roam about, unattached, fluttering like slender pieces of cloth swept by the wind.

The second component in furyu, which can mean "flowing," can also mean "waters" and "to be washed away." Imagine the wind rustling tree leaves above a brook of crystal-clear water. For

Hacho

"Intentional uneven-ness," one phrase for expressing asymmetrical balance, a distinctive feature of Japanese arts. Japanese poetry, for instance, has uneven, asymmetrical numbers of lines per verse—three for haiku and five for waka poems. In Japanese flower arrangement, the application of unevenness is endlessly changeable and calls forth a charismatic feeling of movement and life, a feeling of naturalness.

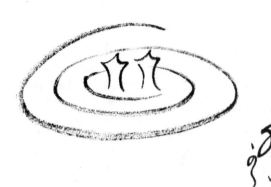

ふるいけや かわずとびこむ みずのおと 飛石

FIG 2.
Furu ike ya \ kawazu tobikomu \ mizu no oto.

"An ancient pond \ a frog leaps— \ the sound of water."

Basho's most famous poem, painted in the style of Kobara Ranseki Sensei.

an instant, the sun shines through the moving leaves, catching a ripple just so, and the glittering water, framed by a mosaic of shadow and light, is extraordinarily beautiful—and then the moment is gone, "washed away" by the changing patterns of light and movement. Furyu describes the heightened awareness of that moment and of the universe that affords a glimpse of that flash of beauty.

Japan has a number of traditional experiences thought to be capable of calling forth the spirit of furyu. Moon viewing and springtime cherry blossom viewing, the contemplation of classical gardens of rock and raked sand—such activities are said to be "furyu experiences." In Japan, those who fail to have such experiences are traditionally thought to be uncultured. Of course there's an important distinction between actually encountering the deep pathos and beauty of creation-destruction in an instant and using the word "furyu," regardless of the actual state of mind, in response to viewing the moon because such an experience is *supposed to be* one of furyu.

56

Furyu is not solely an appreciation for nature; it is also a detached connection with nature. Detachment—the word hints at but does not fully describe the state of mind alluded to here—allows one to connect with all parts of the natural experience and not just aspects commonly assumed to be pleasant. It was this component of furyu that allowed cultured Japanese to sometimes write a poem just before death, which was once a fairly common custom.

Furyu relates to a sensitivity and heightened connection with nature, and it can therefore occur in moments or settings outside its traditional associations. In his book *Tea Life, Tea Mind*, Sen Soshitsu XV, the head of the Urasenke tea school, recalls:

> Once, at the home of an American acquaintance, I found hanging in an open window a pair of metal chopsticks, the kind used for arranging a charcoal fire. When I asked my friend why they were there, I was told, "When the wind blows they strike each other and make the most beautiful sound." I was delightfully amazed; they were his wind bell. A Japanese would never use them in any way other than to handle charcoal, but here they were serving a completely different purpose. This insight was so perfectly furyu that I almost did not take notice of it, and with that realization I experienced a twofold surprise.[9]

The word "furyu" has been used in Japan since the Heian period (794–1192). Unlike other periods in Japanese history, the Heian age was an essentially peaceful one, characterized by a love for the rich, ornate, and elaborate. Yet shadowing this romantic, and at times even pretentious, Heian aesthetic was another, very different way of looking at beauty, one that drew its inspiration from the fleeting, simple magnificence of wind and water—furyu. And although aspects of Heian culture were influenced by Chi-

Haiku

Short poem arranged in three lines of five, seven, and five syllables. A haiku captures the essence of a brief, transient moment in one's life and the universe. The composition of haiku is believed to lead to an enhanced state of sensitivity and closeness to nature.

Hara

Refers to the lower abdomen, a point of mental focus and stabilization from which correct bodily movement originates.

nese civilization and art, furyu appears to be a wholly Japanese concept. It was embraced by the samurai, who, given their at least potentially violent and short-lived existence, were drawn to ideas like mono no aware and furyu. Although furyu dates far back into Japanese history, like many aspects of the Way, it is concurrently ancient and immediate.

In addition to describing the flash of intensity in which time ceases, furyu indicates that we should flow (suggested by "ryu") through life as the wind moves through the myriad aspects of nature, touching everything fully but not clinging to any one thing.

Furyu embraces the ever-changing, fleeting character of life, beauty, and nature. Yet it doesn't imply resignation. Resignation relates to defeat and giving up, and the acceptance contained in furyu is one that takes place when we realize our essential unity with the transient universe, and in this state, there is no defeat, nothing to fight against. In embracing absolute acceptance and harmony with the constantly changing universe, furyu is ultimately positive.

In the Ways, furyu describes an instant in which the mind experiences the poignancy of a brief moment of fragile beauty, a moment so overwhelming and intense that words can barely hint at it—cherry blossoms caught by the wind, and for the briefest moment . . . cascading . . . hanging in a cloud of pink.

Shibumi

Balanced imbalances, artlessness, solitude, antiquity—all are fundamental to classical Japanese sensibilities. They also relate to wabi and sabi, which in turn have a kinship with the concepts *shibumi* ("elegance") and *shibui* ("elegant"). Shibumi also relates to something astringent in taste, while shibui indicates that which is unaffected or refined.

An unripe persimmon is traditionally said to have a shibui taste. In ikebana, a shibui flower arrangement elicits a feeling of coolness during a scorching summer and warmth on a chilly day. Shibumi is quiet and subtle. It is soothing and fulfilling to the soul in a manner unrelated to reasoning. It is the sensibility of "not too much," the use of aesthetic restraint in the highest sense. It is suggested by the English phrase "in good taste," but its reverberations widen and join other Japanese aesthetic and spiritual principles like wabi-sabi.

Shibui and shibumi are artistic ideals that suggest a timeless, beautiful elegance that transcends a particular style or trend. Shibui items aren't showy (in coloration, for example), but rich in quality. Such items are called *shibui-mono*, literally "shibui things." Unpolished silver or gold, or the hue of ashes or bran, can produce an unpretentious, yet elegant and tranquil shibui effect. The classical color arrangement of a woman's kimono, a traditional martial artist's costume of quilted *gi* (cotton garment) and *hakama* (full, skirted pants), the color design of a Japanese guest room, the garments and utensils of the tea ceremony—all evoke shibumi.

Terms that relate to the shibumi ideal are *hade* and *jimi*: If a painting is hade, it is too loud (for example, in color) or even garish. On the other hand, artwork with a naturalistic, subdued, and subtle character is deemed jimi. A piece of calligraphy, an ink painting, or a kimono that is jimi approaches shibumi.

The collection by many Japanese of *suiseki* ("art stones") provides an interesting example of the pursuit of shibumi. Suiseki is the art of symbolizing natural phenomena, from countryside to the universe, using a stone a few inches to a foot or more in dimension. The art begins with the acquisition of stones in nature

Hyoshi

Hyoshi describes "timing" and "rhythm." In the martial Ways, timing is clearly vital. Likewise in shodo, the brushed characters, sitting motionless on the paper, should nevertheless look like they're moving. This is "motion in stillness." Art that displays a visible rhythm in the manner that music gives off an audible rhythm can only be achieved in shodo, and in other Ways like budo and chado, by means of relaxation. Relaxation allows us to achieve calmness in action and action in calmness. We are only able to find timing and rhythm when we stay calm despite outward movement.

GA: *"Graceful elegance."* *Grace, elegance, simplicity, and naturalness are embodied in most Japanese folk crafts and arts. Aesthetic concepts, such as shibumi, also hint at this state of grace.*

and consummates in a sensation of beauty and spiritual connection between the fancier and the stone.

Collectors look for simple lines on their suiseki, since these are evocative of shibumi. Stones shaped like faraway mountains, or *toyama*, and dark-hued stones are also examples of shibui suiseki. Suiseki that have an abundance of shibumi give off a sense of reserve, refinement, and serenity. Shibumi is particularly noticeable in a suiseki's texture. Shibui suiseki have a texture and character marked by understatement.

An authentic niwa garden is another good place to witness a manifested shibumi. Tendencies characteristic of Japanese art and art objects—such as lack of clutter; simple, reserved backdrops and undecorated surfaces; uneven numbers; lower, as opposed to higher, denominations; subtle suggestion; rounded and natural forms—hint at the subtle elegance of shibumi, a quality we can discover by observing nature and direct participation in Japanese classical arts. The similarity of this aesthetic to wabi, sabi, furyu, and others only mirrors the holistic nature of life itself.

Shibumi itself expresses this synthesis. A Japanese aphorism relating to this aesthetic and the use of color states that an artist needs to comprehend only the roles of white, black, and crimson, which form an understated synthesis and ultimately one hue. All other uses of coloration, including the decreasing of strength or graying of tone, will happen naturally with this comprehension. The expression of this adage is seen in brush writing and ink painting where the sole speck of color is a scarlet accent, the signature stamp (*inkan*) of the artist. In the niwa, a similar red accent is found in the *maku*, the felt covering on a viewing bench.

Subtle elegance also arises from suggestion. Although colored ink is common in sumi-e today, traditionally artists used black ink (*sumi*). This monochrome wasn't because of a dislike of color or a lack of comprehension of its use; rather it stemmed from the artists' awareness of the power of elegant suggestion—the power of shibumi. A flower painted purple will be forever purple, but one rendered by a few strokes of ebony ink can be any hue the viewer's imaginativeness solicits. Similarly, a few brush strokes can suggest a flock of birds and a single stroke can indicate a stalk of bamboo.

This shibui aesthetic of suggestion focuses on beginnings and endings, whereas much of Western art concentrates on a "climactic instant." For instance, everyone enjoys a dazzling spray of flowers in full bloom, and the Japanese artist is no different, but in Japanese aesthetics, scarcely opened buds and scattered flower petals resting on the earth are also deeply appreciated. They feature prominently in flower arrangement. And although the climactic moment suggested by fully blooming flowers may be awe-inspiring, it also precludes an opportunity for the elegant engagement of the imagination.

Shizenteki

Shizenteki implies "naturalness," and reverence for nature is a central aspect of Japanese art and traditional culture. Japan is, after all, a country whose inhabitants once sliced holes in the roofs of their farmhouses in order to avoid chopping down a tree. And such farmhouses were often built to fit in the curve of the countryside rather than the other way around.

Ichi-go, Ichi-e

"One encounter, one opportunity." Refers to the emphasis in the Ways on being fully present in the moment based on an awareness of its ephemeral nature. Due to the fleeting nature of each instant, every moment is precious, and it is the only moment that genuinely exists. By focusing on the past or the future, and only encountering the present fully during times such as a crisis situation, we sleepwalk through life. The Ways emphasize activities that require the full, unified force of the mind and body—a force brought to bear in the present and in a flash.

Nonetheless, Japanese art is more than the mere celebration and preservation of nature. Ikebana, for example, isn't simply the appreciation of flowers in their natural state; no, the flowers are clipped, bent, positioned—they are arranged—in a manner that embraces their natural tendencies *but also recognizes the natural artistic tendencies of the artist.*

Japanese people, like people everywhere, love forests and flowers. Yet, if you visit a Japanese garden, you won't see a spontaneous grouping of trees, but a meticulous arrangement of them in the garden. And, although arranged, the grouping appears unforced and beautiful. The arrangement appears unaffected and artless, but there is something more.

A bonsai tree offers a good example. We marvel at how the bonsai seems like a replication of a tree in nature, only in miniature. But if we look longer and more carefully at an exquisite bonsai, we note a curious fact: *the tree looks more distinctive and striking than a tree in nature.*

A distinctively twisted, aged, and yet beautiful tree can be found in nature, but not often, and this same tree, only dwarfed, while found occasionally growing from a crag in some remote wilderness, is rarer still.

Bonsai (and suiseki) thus isn't simply nature as it is; it is nature in a super concentrated form, a form that is squeezed, compacted, and multiplied in intensity. In the case of bonsai, and even ikebana and other crafts, we can think of Japanese art as nature reinterpreted and intensified, a distillation of its essential quality.

Thus, the painstaking pruning and wiring of bonsai are not meant to reproduce nature as it is but to produce something beyond what is usually found in nature: simply to copy nature pales in comparison. It is when the life force and creativity of the artist—the human being as a functioning part of nature—merge with the essence and rhythm of nature that something wondrous results. That result is art—not Japanese art—but art.

Although not alone in this recognition, Japan has refined it over centuries to a high level. Japanese art has united an awareness of nature with an innate predilection for formally established ways of doing things. These established forms, or *kata*, are widespread, but their

ONOZUKARA:
Brushed in the cursive sosho style of the monk Chiei, this character can mean "self" when pronounced ji and "naturally" or "naturalness" when pronounced onozukara or inozuto. Naturalness lies at the heart of all the Japanese Ways. And in these Ways, the individual self and nature are not separate.

use accords with the idea of shizenteki. (I say more about kata later in the book.) Although Japanese art has specific, long-established rules that contribute to its recognizably Japanese style, these rules generally work within the natural order.

The ideal of asymmetry is one example. Just as flowers do not grow in neat rows in the wilderness, symmetry is avoided in a Japanese garden or in ikebana. Nature is "arranged" in the traditional Japanese arts, but the arrangement accords with the intrinsic movement of ki in nature. Thus, in general an ikebana artist will bend a flower, but not so much that it will be forced into a shape it would not exhibit in nature.

Relating to this idea is *sashiai*, which can be unsatisfactorily translated as "reciprocal interference." Sashiai embodies the idea that less is more. By reduction and elimination, by leaving certain elements of a design empty, specific aspects of nature can more successfully be brought to the viewer's attention. For instance, it is common to find in the small hut used in the tea ceremony a simple, seasonal arrangement of flowers. Wandering through the garden leading to the hut, you are likely to notice something unusual—no flowers. This deliberate act of reduction and elimination serves to heighten the effect of viewing the few flowers sim-

Ikebana

*Literally "living flow-
ers." Refers to the tra-
ditional art of flower
arrangement. Also
known as kado (the
Way of flowers), its
origins are in Buddhist
floral offerings.*

ply yet carefully displayed in the hut. It concentrates attention on them, and expresses the essence of the garden itself and even the character of flowers as a whole. Using less to intensify an effect, and intensify it in harmony with nature, is the essence of sashiai.

The same effect can be observed in ink painting. A large blank area may be left in a painting. But this void isn't really emp-ty; it is filled with itself and defines, for example, the small figure wandering up a mountain path, surrounded by vast emptiness. In sumi-e, the deliberate absence of form actually supports the struc-ture of the painting and draws attention to specific parts of the painting.

Sashiai leads to *mitate*, a new manner of seeing. Many of us just glance at the world, usually through the eyes of the past, and in the example above, the absence of flowers in the garden leading to the the tea hut encourages observers to genuinely see and con-nect with the flowers in the arrangement. With the mitate that comes from sashiai, the observer is able to make a deep, immedi-ate, and intimate connection with specific aspects of nature that have been arranged by the artist. Ultimately, it is a connection with the universe itself.

In some ways, this reverence for nature has entered the realm of mysticism, a "natural mysticism," as certain Western scholars have stated, as opposed to a "spiritual mysticism" con-ceived in a Judeo-Christian context. In this natural mysticism, nature isn't perceived as merely plants and animals, as something bestowed on humankind by a separate Creator. It is essentially a nondualistic perception in which nature is the visible aspect of the Creator on earth, part of the Creator in the same way that legs are part of the body and not separate from it. Nature is perhaps better described as the Creator himself/herself, as the absolute, or the absolute universe.

Thus, in the Do, oneness with nature is more than harmony

with the natural physical environment; it is union with the absolute universe itself. But shizenteki in the Ways implies still more than this. It means to embody natural principles in the way we function, and this embodiment can occur in any environment—urban or naturalistic. It isn't about *where we are* but *what we are,* and how we act. (More discussion of shizenteki and the concept of naturalness is in chapter 3.)

We practice one of the Do to reveal for ourselves and to ourselves the principles inherent in nature. In the Way of the flower, the classical strata are heaven, earth, and humanity. Certain elements will represent heaven, or perhaps God, others the earth, and still others, branches for example, humankind. Humans are placed between heaven and earth in kado, not only as an intermediary but also as a means for us to absorb the teachings of the universe itself. The same can be said for other Ways, and in studying such Ways we have a chance to directly and intimately experience and experiment with the principles of the universe in a microcosm.

Ma

More than an aesthetic standard, *ma* specifies a technical principle inherent in many of the Japanese arts and Ways. Ma means "interval" or "space." In budo, or the martial Ways, ma (or *ma-ai*) refers to a proper combative distance. The person that controls the distance and space in combat controls the entire encounter. Position yourself too close and the opponent can strike you at will, without even having to take a step (Figure 3). Remain too far away and no sense of connection with the opponent is possible. Furthermore, no combatant will intelligently attack from across the room. In many systems of jujutsu, aiki-jujutsu, and aikido, the fundamental ma-ai is one in which the opponent can't hit

FIG. 3. A ma-ai (distance) in jujutsu that is too close.

or kick you without having taken at least one step. This distance can be roughly gauged as that at which the fingertips of two extended arms just barely touch (Figure 4), and a similar distance is used in Japanese swordsmanship, in which the sword tips nearly touch (Figure 5). By having to step in to attack, the assailant is forced to commit to the assault, and he also must make a larger, slower movement, which tends to "telegraph" the attack. Ma is thus of vital importance in budo. Not too close, not too far away.

This idea of just the right distance also applies in human relationships. The sort of closeness expected and welcomed from an intimate would likely be deemed uncomfortable from an acquaintance or stranger. Appropriate physical and psychological distance thus obviously varies according to the person and circumstances. This is also true in the martial arts, where we might stand closer than the standard ma if we feel that an opponent isn't especially skilled, but move farther apart than usual when dealing with a particularly fast and powerful attacker.

That a highly developed awareness of ma would have evolved in Japan is easily understood once we consider its geographical and

FIG. 4. A ma-ai (distance) in jujutsu that is correct (where the fingertips just touch).

FIG. 5. A ma-ai (distance) in kenjutsu that is correct (where the sword tips nearly touch).

historical circumstances. Japan is a small island nation that has long been densely populated. Over the centuries, if for no other reason than to avoid conflict, the Japanese had to cultivate a sense of ma, had to literally "give each other some space." But, despite the crowdedness of the environment, the aim was not to keep others away, which would have adversely affected group cohesion in this group-oriented culture; rather, correct ma embodies space but not excessive distance, and it will vary by person and situation in both martial and social relationships.

Each of us gives off a certain "presence." We say that some people have a big presence, whereas others do not. And this presence, like ma, varies according to time and situation. For instance, we often note that actors appear larger on stage than off stage. This is said to be due to the fact that they're projecting to the audience during a performance. The big presence that is projected is sometimes described in Japan as ki, "life energy" or "spiritual force." A dynamic, positive mental state gives rise to a powerful outward expansion of ki—a big presence. Conversely, a negative, withdrawn state of mind creates a concurrent withdrawal of ki. Thus, from moment to moment, situation to situation, the radiation of ki modulates.

Correct ma can be imagined if we think of two people as magnets, each with an aura of magnetic force. If we gradually bring the positive ends of each magnet toward each other, we can get an impression of ma. When the magnets are too far apart, we can't feel the magnetic aura, but at the right distance we can perceive the two fields of force touch. This is correct ma. Likewise, if we force the two magnets past this point, too close, they start to push away from each other. Where magnets give off magnetic energy, people give off ki. Ki is sensed through the hara, a natural and immovable center inside human beings. The concepts of ki and hara are explored at greater length in chapter 3, which examines the spiritual aspects of the Ways, but it's important to note here that ma pertains to both the body and the spirit.

Ma can also be seen in Japanese visual arts such as shodo. The brush strokes that form a character must not be too far apart

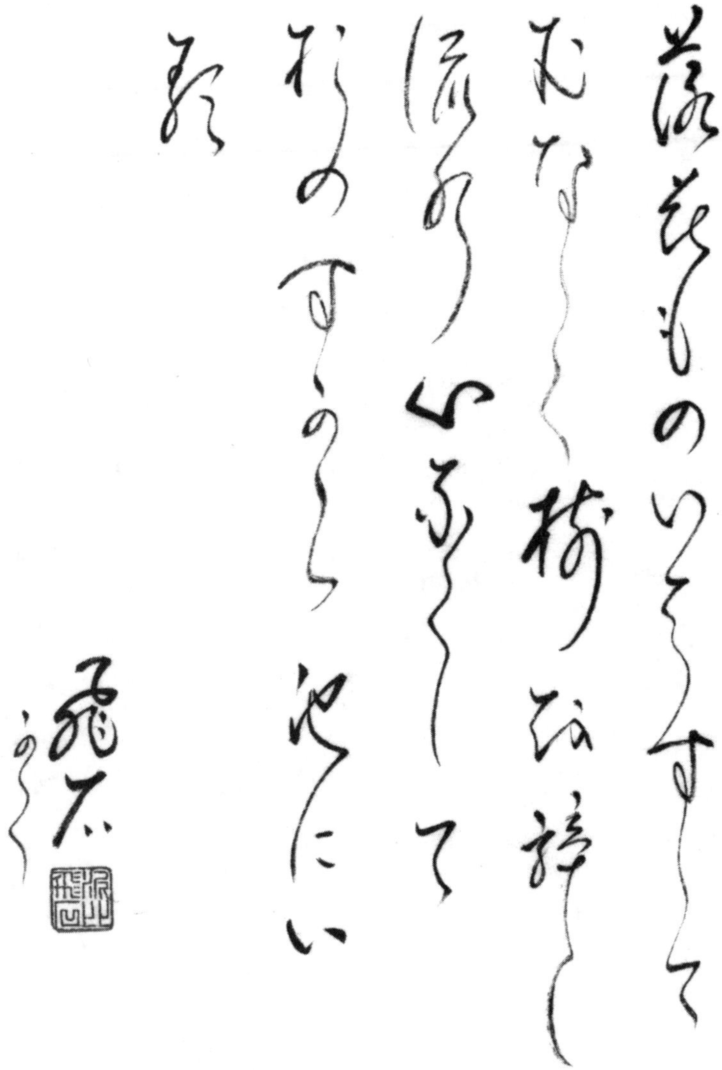

FIG. 6.
Rakka monoiwazu shite / munashiku ju o jishi / ryu sui kokoro / nakushite onozukara / ike ni iru.

"The falling flowers say not a single word. / they're spent as they leave the treetops. / Disappearing into the flowing water without hesitation, / they spontaneously drift into the pond."

This ancient poem from the *Wakanroeishu* is painted with a *fujidana* arrangement. It describes the accord with nature and the acceptance of life's natural process that lie at the heart of the Ways.

or it will not hold together, and placing the strokes too close to each other only creates a cramped feeling. Similarly, the space between characters should be not too close nor too far—just like people in society. In the same vein, the lines of a poem must connect with each other in a harmonious way. When a poem is to be written in uniform, vertical lines, it is called *fujidana* in design, and a correct ma is relatively easy to arrive at (Figure 6). However, when a *chirashi*, or "scattered," arrangement is used to create

69

FIG. 7.

Omoi demo / Hakanaki mono wa / Fuku kaze no / Oto ni mo kikanu / Koi ni zo arikeru.

"It's ever fleeting, / like the echoing wind's voice, / that's no longer heard. / Love only truly exists / In the flash of the moment."

This poem from the *Nishi Honganji Sanjuroku Nin Shu* aptly sums up Japanese attitudes to impermanence and reflects elements of mono no aware and ichi-go, ichi-e.

asymmetrical balance, ma is much more challenging (Figure 7). Note that in Figure 7 I've painted the characters to form more than one "island." If the groupings are too close, they cease to function as islands and run together. Too far apart, on the other hand, and there is a lack of cohesion. The ki of each grouping must touch but not repel. Thus, the sense of ma and of balance in shodo are intimately connected.

In sumi-e, the lines applied by the brush are frequently incomplete. The incompleteness allows the mind's eye to complete the composition, thus drawing the observer into the work. In this minimalist approach, the empty space is important. This space is ma. In Western painting empty space is designated "negative space," and students are usually urged to "fill up the space." But in Japanese visual arts, from sumi-e to flower arrangement, empty space isn't seen as something negative. I often advise people interested in Japanese calligraphy to look at the white space instead of the lines of black ink when copying sample characters. When I engage in brush writing, I regularly think of outlining the white space as opposed to drawing lines on blank paper. Ma is space, but the space isn't empty.

In-Yo

In and *yo* are commonly known in the West by their Chinese equivalents, *yin* and *yang*. Their origins are related to Taoism, in which they refer to the basic, complementary, and inseparable dualism that is evidenced in the relative world.

In the *Tao Te Ching*, the canon of Taoism, Lao-tzu described yin and yang thus:

> Is and is not are mutually arising;
> Difficult and easy are complementary;
> Long and short arise from comparison;
> Higher and lower are interdependent;
> Vocalization and verbalization harmonize with
> each other;
> Before and after accompany each other.[10]

Although the Chinese origins of yin and yang are well known, few realize that ancient Japan offered parallels in its native Shintoism. In Shinto mythology, at a moment before time, the

Inro

The classical Japanese apparel, the kimono, had no pockets. A sash tied the robes together. Objects carried were held on a cord tucked under the sash. The hanging objects (sage-mono) were secured with carved toggles (netsuke). A sliding bead (ojime) was strung on the cord between the netsuke and the sagemono to bind or slacken the opening of the sage-mono. The best known accessory was the inro, a little box used for carrying medica-tion and seals. Inro are beautiful art objects that are still carved and widely collected. See also netsuke.

universe existed as an undifferentiated whole, without form or substance, absolute life energy (ki) that contained no dualistic or relative aspects—pure oneness. Suddenly, by means of a spiral movement, the ki of the universe began to divide, with one aspect swirling centrifugally upward to become heaven and the other corkscrewing downward with infinite centripetal force to form the earth. Into this swirling mass of ki were born Izanagi and Izanami, male and female kami, divine entities, whose birth herald-ed the creation of the relative world. Duality manifests throughout Shintoism.

Thus, in Japan in and yo and their origins in native Shinto and Taoism have, among other influences, formed the contempo-rary cultural matrix. The concept of in and yo, although clearly discernible in Taoism and Shinto, is in fact a universal one, embodying the essence of existence itself.

In-yo, preferably linked rather than split by "and," literally describes "light" and "dark." Since we can recognize light only because of dark, and vice versa, in-yo cannot be separated. Oppo-sites—front, back; up, down; heads, tails—can be known only in relation to one another. Heads and tails are inseparable parts of the same coin, which is ultimately the universe itself. And though opposites, they are not in conflict.

Attempts to ultimately and fully divide aspects of existence are doomed to end in failure, delusion, and discord. The absolute—and that is the key word—universe is one, and its essence is ki—or God, kami, the universe, nature, etc., whatever might be preferred. While this absolute ki has divided to form the world in which we live, our relative, dualistic world is never sepa-rate from the absolute universe. It is, rather, a manifestation of it. This is expressed by the Zen phrase, "not one, not two."

In-yo is not one, not two, and this holds true for all parts of reality. In-yo makes the absolute, undifferentiated nature of the universe visible, just as distinct phonemes make language possible. Mind and body are one, for instance, and discerning where one ends and the other begins is impossible. Nevertheless, we still speak of mind *and* body, since communication requires such distinctions. We must, however, realize that speech is an artificial construct that mimics nature; it isn't nature itself, and words are not the things they describe.

Moreover, if the two parts of in-yo are not separate and not separable, then they point to something with apparent dual parts that are actually linked "beneath the surface." That something is our relative world. And in the relative world, we see up/down, rich/poor, gentle/severe—endless dichotomy. In seeing these opposites, it's easy to conclude that life is conflict.

A more encompassing view allows us to glimpse the source of these opposites, and the fact that they cannot exist apart from each other. With this observation comes the realization that all opposites form a single whole that is the absolute ki of the universe.

What's more, just as the dual aspect of life does not negate its underlying oneness, seeing this oneness does not eliminate the relative nature of our world. To believe that only harmony exists is a worldview that is flawed, just as is the belief that conflict between opposites is the nature of life. Neither assertion is complete, and both ideas are based on a dualistic viewpoint that engenders conflict in and of itself.

Looking at one aspect of human nature, men and women represent opposites. But these opposites are complementary, thus the natural attraction between them. A specific man and woman join to create a child. From two, we have one; and from the dual, we move to the singular. This child, male or female, finds its opposite. From one, we return to duality. These two in turn give birth to a child. And duality becomes one again.

Not one, not two. This is the essence of existence, the comprehension of which has a revolutionary effect on human consciousness.

Funi

D. T. Suzuki, lecturer and writer on Zen, often spoke of "the One in the All and the All in the One." He stated that in this seemingly simple phrase could be found the essence of Zen and Japanese art. Haiku authority Yoel Hoffman has written of the "haiku moment," a nondualistic moment in which the separation between subject and object, self and other, grows blurred. Everything is revealed as it is, for in well-crafted haiku the moment is now, time and place cease to exist, becoming any time and every place.

In a similar vein, Yanagi Soetsu, author of *The Unknown Craftsman*, expounded on a quality known as *funi*:

> What, then, is Enlightenment? It is the state of being free from all duality. Sometimes the term "Oneness" is used, but "Non-dual Entirety" (funi) is a more satisfactory term because Oneness is likely to be construed as the opposite of duality and hence understood in relative terms.[11]

Funi is a term that may stem from Japanese Buddhism. In its aboriginal Sanskrit, it is *advaitam*, and it is found in the Yuima Sutra. But its relationship to the Japanese arts and Ways goes beyond specific religious affiliation.

In funi, or nonduality, the Creator and the created can be distinguished from one another, but they cannot ultimately be divided. Likewise, in the Japanese Ways the artist and the created art

In-Yo

Japanese equivalent of Chinese yin and yang, a Taoist concept that refers to the basic, complementary, and inseparable dualism evidenced in the relative world.

cannot be separated. Nonduality, in fact, is more than a Japanese artistic construct and hints at the genuine nature of existence, which transcends cultural and relative distinctions. Funi then points to a state in which the division between ourselves and others, between life and death, dissolves. And with the dissolving of duality comes the transcendence of fear as well as conflict of every kind.

In relation to the Japanese arts and Ways, funi is the lack of separation between what we in the West might typically think of as beauty and what we perceive as ugliness. Japanese art regularly includes asymmetry and irregularity. Embodied by the wabi-sabi concept, this inclusion of the "imperfect" in the Japanese aesthetic of beauty is, at least potentially, an expression of the unity of opposites, an expression of nonduality. In such a case, beauty is not the opposite of ugliness. Rather, beauty lies in a state beyond and includes all opposites; beauty is thus found in naturalness.

For the artist in harmony with nature, no effort or contrivance is needed to produce wabi-sabi elegance. Existing in a state transcending distinction, a state in which the duality separating the artist and the universe has dissolved, the artist allows the ki of nature to flow through her or him and into the art being created. Nature, the artist, and the creation form a "nondual entirety." The result is a beauty that does not distinguish between ugliness and its opposite.

Ichi-go, Ichi-e

Ichi-go, ichi-e means "one encounter, one opportunity." It emphasizes that every second is alive and moving; it does not stay in place and it doesn't last. Because of its ephemeral nature, every moment is precious—it is the only moment that genuinely exists.

Judo

The Way of yielding and pliability, a modern martial sport founded by Kano Jigoro Sensei in 1882.

By focusing on the past or the future and encountering the present fully only during times of great intensity, such as a crisis situation, we sleepwalk through life. In the Ways, from tea ceremony to the martial arts, there is an emphasis on the full, unified force of the mind and body, a force brought to bear in the present and in a flash.

In ink painting, for instance, owing to the variable character of the paper, brush, and ink, it's not possible to know exactly how the bristles will twist or turn in contact with the paper or how much ink the paper will absorb. Depending on these variables, sometimes the brush must move more quickly and sometimes more slowly. And judgments must be made as the changing conditions are observed; adjustments must be made right then and there. The artwork that results is one of a kind, as is the singular instant that produced each action in its creation. An exact reproduction is impossible.

Moreover, in shodo and sumi-e "touching up" or redrawing aren't allowed. Erasing isn't possible. The only option is to adapt to the moment at hand, as it takes place, and if things don't go as planned, the sole choice is to move forward. You can't go backward or stop the flow of events, and "do overs" don't exist.

If this sounds a lot like life, it is not a coincidence, and this parallel is one of the ways that the various Do function as lessons in the art of living. The Do are tools to help us see into our nature and the nature of living. When properly practiced, they offer a device to help us wake up to the essence of life, to realize that living is now or not at all.

Ichi-go, ichi-e as a concept also gives the Japanese arts some of their distinctive "Japaneseness," or perhaps the unique character of these arts has given rise to ichi-go, ichi-e. Regardless, the mutual influence is profound, and it serves to distinguish Japanese art from its Western counterpart. For example, where sumi-e is based on a quick, simple brush stroke that is not preceded by a sketch and cannot be touched up later, European oil painting is often built up, altered, and repainted until the desired result is obtained. As the artist and creation are one, this difference represents more than a variance in technique. In sumi-e, we see the spirit of ichi-go, ichi-e directly manifested as technique.

Another example of ichi-go, ichi-e can be found in the martial Ways of Japan. Budo is derived from the hoary traditions of the *bushi*, the warrior of feudal Japan. For a bushi—or more familiarly known as a samurai—facing death was an everyday consideration. The bushi's life was likened to the cherry blossom, whose vibrant color and beauty remain only briefly before being scattered by the wind. Bound to give his life in the service of his homeland, clan, and lord, the bushi knew that he could be required to lay down his life, without faltering, at a moment's notice. By resolving to live each day as if it were his last, he discovered how to experience life completely, without indecisiveness or regret.

For the bushi to be able to have a positive attitude in the face of possibly imminent death, he learned not to worry about either the past, or particularly, the future. This ability is also indispensable for the modern student of the Ways. If the mind remains in the now, it's impossible to worry. People worry solely about an event that's come to pass or one that may take place in the future; the current moment contains no time or space for worry.

The past is forever unalterable, and fretting over the future weakens our ability to fully grasp the present moment and could even condemn us to live through an event twice, first in the imagination and again in reality.

Keeping the mind in the now, unless we consciously want to contemplate the past or future, it's possible to face life without fear. There are then no thoughts of past failure or future hurt, and a positive mental state results: fudoshin, the "immovable mind."

Jujutsu

The art of yielding and pliability, Japan's oldest martial art, used by feudal warriors as a minimally armed form of combat.

Five Attributes of the Way

HARMONY

Harmony underlies the Ways. In kado, for example, you must understand the character and growth patterns of the plants you're working with. Yet mere comprehension of the temperament of a given flower isn't enough to arrive at wa, or harmony, in ikebana.

The tranquillity and directness of a flower are mirrored in the eye of the artist, once she surrenders to its blossoms. The scalloped edge of the mountains in the distance, if they can be seen from a window, should be in harmony with the flower arrangement inside the home. The season, too, should be brought into the composition in ikebana, and the artist's ki and creativity are linked to this to give birth to a harmonious trinity. Structure and hue, blossoms and branches, buds and foliage combine with the vase and home, the time of year, and the ki of the adept. Harmony is attained in kado through a refined composite of understanding and reverence. This harmonious condition is reflected in the kado expert's relaxed and gentle treatment of flowers, even when shaping their stems.

Similarly, the more accomplished one becomes in the Japanese martial Ways, the greater the ability to recognize and understand an opponent's intentions. Through correct, hard training, the martial artist arrives at an unflappable alertness that allows him to literally comprehend the opponent's very mind. Nevertheless, this enhanced sensitivity is insignificant unless it is accompanied by a spirit that respects the opponent's intentions. Forcing people in budo, or plants in kado, seldom equals a practical or efficient use of ki. When both understanding and respect coalesce, harmony is brought about in budo; and in this harmonious state, an expert can lead and control an assailant.

Harmony is a critical aspect of brush writing as well. In shodo, harmony is expressed through dynamic balance. Balance is asymmetrical, which causes a feeling of action within the characters. It could be likened to a photograph of a sprinter, whose inclined running stance has been frozen by the camera. The snapshot gives a sensation of motion (as opposed to one of a person standing still). But this feeling of movement is unlike that in a photo taken of a runner at the moment she has tripped and is stumbling forward. Both images show bodies in motion; the crucial difference between the two is balance.

Dynamic balance in shodo is also achieved through a natural variation of heavy and light brush pressure, which produces a fluctuation of thick and thin lines of ink. Brush strokes of uniform thickness create a work that is awkward, artificial, and dead.

Although harmony is expressed differently in kado, budo, and shodo, the principle of harmony is a constant element in all the Ways.

ASYMMETRICAL BALANCE

Asymmetrical balance is another distinctive feature of the Japanese arts. It is sometimes known as *hacho*, intentional unevenness, which is an especially distinctive feature of Japanese culture. Japanese poetry, to give just one example, has an uneven number of asymmetrical lines of verse, three lines of five, seven, and five syllables in haiku and five lines of five, seven, five, seven, and seven syllables in waka poems.

Asymmetrical balance can also be clearly seen in kado, where it elicits a feeling of naturalness. Since nature itself is ever changing, kado shuns a dead, static impression, which is precisely what is produced by rigid, symmetrical balance. Unevenness suggests endless change and evokes a feeling of charismatic movement

Kan

Intuitive perception; also connotes the idea of "quickened insight," the ability to perceive what is about to take place even before, for example, all the action has played out. In the Ways, it refers to learning through direct experience, personal discovery, and intuition, and by means of the cultivation of heightened intuitive perception itself.

79

Kan Geiko

Rigorous training in one of the Do that deliberately takes place during the coldest time of the year. While it can be misinterpreted as an exercise in masochism, kan geiko is actually a form of "spiritual forging"—a quality commonly identified as one of the primary reasons for participating in the various Do forms. The Do value and cultivate a positive and indomitable attitude, the real motivation for training long hours with no heat in the dead of winter. See also shochu geiko.

and life. Thus, a relatively long branch placed on one side of an arrangement will not be balanced on the other by a matching branch; rather, something exhibiting a contrasting texture or shape will be used to create a dynamic, asymmetrical balance. Kado also uses in particular an unequal triangular balance. Many compositions consist of three central elements that represent heaven (*ten*), earth (*chi*), and humankind (*jin*), with humankind assuming an intermediate balance between the other two.

"The Way of flowers" also makes ample use of empty space, which tempts the mind's eye to complete the arrangement, drawing the observer into the work. In other words, the incomplete asks to be completed; that which is unfinished is in harmony with life's dynamics of unchanging change and evolution. This expression of asymmetry does not inevitably denote a lack of balance; rather, in kado, the union of opposites creates a form of balanced imbalance. An unbalanced balance in kado mirrors the nature of a Zen koan, a metaphysical question that rises above the conditions of logical thought.

The manipulation of asymmetry, incompleteness, and unevenness are also found in Japanese ink painting, brush writing, and even classical architecture. Like harmony, asymmetry is a ubiquitous feature of the Ways.

ARTLESSNESS

As discussed earlier, the Ways have been influenced by philosophies and religions that include Zen and other forms of Buddhism, Shinto, and Dokyo. In the Ways and Taoism, less is more, and noninterference with nature allows the creative course of the universe to flow through the artist.

In order to grasp the concept of artlessness, an understanding of aesthetics such as wabi and sabi is necessary.

As stated previously, the poverty of wabi is, in the tea cere-mony for example, a poverty of ostentatious display and the human attachment to things; it speaks to the suspension of intel-lectual entanglement and all forms of self-regard and affectation in the pursuit of the unadorned truth of nature underlying all relative phenomena. As nature is asymmetrical, spontaneous, imperfect, wabi expresses a purity of natural imperfection. It evokes the nobility of artlessness, of even "deformity." When this artlessness merges with a simple antiqueness, Japanese artists describe this as sabi. In certain instances sabi, literally "solitariness," suggests an effortless quality.

The aesthetic concepts of wabi, sabi, and shibumi underlie and inform the ideal of artlessness in the Japanese Ways, but they also, at their deepest level, touch something in the human heart that is universal.

Karate-do

"The Way of the emp-ty hand," a Japanese martial Way imported from Okinawa that emphasizes striking techniques and is often practiced competitively.

IMPERMANENCE

Sabi also relates to the universal impermanence in life; it expresses the fleeting nature of existence. To blend sabi into life is to recognize that relationships, even those we cherish, are fleeting. They exist in the moment, and once this is seen with our whole heart, every moment becomes precious, stretching beyond the boundaries of time.

Sabi as an expression of impermanence in art means that, whether we participate in cha-no-yu, view another's flower arrangement, or create our own arrangements, the mind must be in the present, knowing we will never again have the chance to encounter that moment.

Not only sabi but indeed all the aesthetic principles of the Ways describe, in their different emphases, a universal Way. Each Do represents a different path to the same spot. Proponents of the

Kata

Traditional, formal exercises designed to preserve and communicate the essential principles of an art. Kata are found in some form in most Japanese arts.

Japanese arts universally regard transience as a respected aesthetic, if not spiritual, element. Releasing self-consciousness and completely experiencing a single, fleeting moment is equal to the realization that life exists only at this instant, and we'll never have another chance to live it again.

Utsuroi is another word that relates to the impermanent nature of the universe. It suggests the ephemeral quality that exists like a reflection in a mirror . . . appearing one second, and disappearing the next . . . with nary a trace left on the reflective surface. It describes in kado, for example, the understanding on the part of the artist and viewer of the profound meaning and beauty inherent in the impermanence of the flowers in an arrangement. Think of the gossamer colors of falling petals. People who see futility in the careful composition of flowers that will soon shrivel and die miss this understanding and suffer under the illusion that some form of everlasting art exists.

The acknowledgment and expression of impermanence is found in many aspects of Japanese culture. Historically, straw sandals were worn out and traded at each stage of a lengthy trip. Clothing often consisted of a small number of widths of cloth loosely sewn together for wearing, and later unsewn for washing. In the traditional house, paper shoji panels were re-covered twice each year. Likewise, straw tatami mats were renewed each autumn. These and other examples reveal the Japanese comfort with impermanence.

Impermanence, nonattachment, living in the present, uniting mind and body in a moment transcending time—all find expression in such aesthetic ideas as the solitude of sabi and the "sentimental melancholy" associated with mono no aware (or simply, *aware*), ideas that make Japanese art clearly unique but that, at the same time, point to something transcendent: creation and destruction each leading inevitably to the other, the never-ending dance of in-yo, the unborn and undying indivisible absolute that lies within the eternal pulse of life and death.

UNITY WITH THE UNIVERSE

Awareness of our inborn unity with the universe or nature is the common point that ties the above principles together. Human beings are no more disconnected from the universe than a wave is independent of the sea. Each wave is unique, and exists, if only for a moment, but every wave originates in the sea, rises from it, and returns to it. The sea and its wave are one.

In like manner, humans are one with the universe. We contain the essential mark of the universe, ki, within us; each individual is a microcosm of the universe. But to know this basic unity requires going beyond hearing or reading of it. You cannot feel the wind by reading about it; further, a theoretical understanding alone, without firsthand experience, without authentic embodiment, only encourages a split between mind and body, a conflict in which the mind "knows" but the body cannot do. It leads to a phantom of comprehension instead of harmony with an absolute universe that is timeless and infinite. In this state of harmony, we directly perceive our own limitless and eternal nature. As between the sea and its wave, harmony with the universe means no beginning, no end, no fear, and no suffering. It is a moment that is unending, beyond the bonds of time, beyond duality.

Harmony in kado, for instance, is arrived at when the artist perceives the growth patterns and attributes of the plants that are being arranged. It is a perception, however, of not only the character of particular plants and flowers used in a flower arrangement but also, on a deeper level, the spirit, or ki, of nature itself.

In bonsai, suiseki, and the arrangement of a traditional garden, Japanese art aims to capture the essential nature of tree,

Keiko

"Practice," but not practice as we think of it in Western terms. Practice in the Do isn't a matter of "beginning a course," or "taking a class." Instead, students of the Ways run through actions that they have repeated hundreds of times in the past. Learning takes place, but frequently on subconscious and intuitive levels.

stone, landscape, to create a work of art that exemplifies the very core of these things, and ultimately, the substance of nature itself. This aim begins with a recognition of the fundamental character of the thing the artist is working with and progresses to a "sculpting" of the material to intensify the expression of its intrinsic character. A Japanese gardener works "with the grain," and as he prunes and shapes, he reveals an aspect of beauty that is born in nature but that nature has hidden in its abundance.

Japanese art aims to discern and then liberate what has always been present. And who are we to assume that such liberation is needed? Humanity is a part of nature. We, like the flowers in ikebana and the trees or shrubs in the niwa, are part of the infinite variety that is the universe. We are transitory and timeless, existing in the eternal present, just like the aspects of nature we create with. In perceiving and freeing aspects of nature that have always existed, we ultimately see into our own nature.

In Japan, native arts both humble and dignify their participants. Humankind is forced to recognize its mortality and the fact of impermanence. But in seeing our smallness in the universe, we discover our link to something infinitely large, eternal, and awesome.

Such ideas aren't always directly articulated in Japan, but they are, and have been, present in most Japanese arts and Ways. They are living notions passed down for generations, and as part of a living tradition these ideas are subject to wide variance of expression, interpretation, and even understanding. Still, they have existed in Japan nearly as long as nature itself.

As an expression of humankind's inseparable interdependence with the universe, the principles described here form an aesthetic independent of a style or trend tied to a certain point in Japanese history. They actually mirror the perpetual character of nature. To comprehend harmony, artlessness, and impermanence is never-ending, much like the endless universe itself; and sincere understanding comes as we bring to light as well as reflect these states in ourselves.

Culture versus the Essence of the Way

It is widely recognized that the various Do (despite having been influenced by Chinese culture, art, and religion) originated in Japan. Because they are inextricably entwined with Japanese culture, an understanding of Japanese culture is needed to make more than superficial progress in their practice. This book was written to aid both writer and reader in arriving at this understanding.

Nevertheless, it is legitimate to ask to what degree the Ways and Japanese culture are separate, can be separated, and indeed if they should be separated. The evidence of neglect on the part of both Western and Japanese students of the Ways to deeply consider these questions makes such an inquiry even more important. In this book we are concerned with two entities: the different Japanese Ways and the Way itself. The Way means the Way of the universe, and so it clearly is not limited to a specific art. The Way is universal; the Ways are particular. Being both simple and complex, this distinction is sometimes overlooked. In a sense, it can and cannot be made. As the mind cannot truly be separated from the body, the Way and Ways cannot be separated. Still, the mind and body have different characteristics and modes of functioning; the mind has no form, the body has form, and so on. We can make distinctions and speak in terms of mental versus physical despite the fundamental oneness of the two. The Way of the universe and its outward expressions, the different Ways, are similarly inseparable but nonetheless distinguishable.

Most people who have practiced a Do seriously have, from

Kendo

The Way of the sword, a modern martial Way centering on the use of the Japanese sword and often practiced as a sport.

85

Kenjutsu

The art of the sword, a martial art based on the classical use of the Japanese sword.

time to time, heard a Japanese teacher state that only a native Japanese practitioner of chado, shodo, budo, and others, can really understand the art. This sentiment, which seems to be less frequently voiced these days, is obviously infuriating to non-Japanese students of the Do. And while this may shock and further infuriate such individuals, I would agree with it—but only on one level.

The Ways are Japanese cultural arts. The Way is not. As Japanese cultural disciplines, the different Do are an outgrowth of Japanese art, history, religion, geography, government, and many other specific factors. And the reference is not simply to contemporary Japanese culture but includes everything that has come before. If we separate the Do from their cultural ground, they cease to exist, degenerating into nothing but a generic sort of art. While multiculturalism is a popular idea and a good thing in general, there is no value in reducing the art forms of other cultures to whatever an individual practitioner is comfortable with based on his own cultural preferences. This kind of homogenizing will only render the arts of other cultures bland and shallow.

The Americanizing of cuisines from other traditions provides a simple example. I like spicy food, and so I frequent Thai restaurants. I'm often disappointed, however, when I discover the food is bland and inauthentic. Querying owners, I'm usually informed that the cuisine has been "adjusted to American tastes." Perhaps, but it has also sometimes been rendered unrecognizable and tasteless. I'd hate to see this happen to the Japanese Do.

Since the Do are an outgrowth of centuries of Japanese cultural development, they can never be understood by Westerners in the manner that native Japanese understand them. Plainly, Westerners aren't Japanese, and we must arrive at our own comprehension of these arts. Whether our comprehension of these arts is problematic depends on whether it results in a homogenization, or "dumbing down," of these classical arts. Like tampering with a rare classic car to make it "look cool" or painting big numbers on an antique clock to make it easier to read, facile alterations to these arts would damage their integrity. And make no mistake, a number of the Do forms are very much "living antiques" that derive part of their value from their antiquity. I, and a number of other Western and Japanese devotees of the Do, would urge Westerners to leave them intact, and if this isn't palatable, to consider a different activity more suitable to their tastes, rather than destroying venerable cultural artifacts.

Despite some Japanese arts and Ways having survived for centuries, as living arts, they are fragile and depend for their survival on the people who teach them. If these people, Japanese or non-Japanese, lose the art's essence that is rooted in Japan, then a given art may be rendered unrecognizable within a generation or two.

What with the westernization and internationalization of Japan, and the transplantation of the Do onto foreign soil, this consideration becomes vital. How will the Do grow outside of Japan? This and other crucial questions need to be looked into, but they form a topic that is beyond the scope of this book. Nonetheless, regarding the successful transplantation of the Do, we need to consider the following ideas.

I now and then hear some American teachers of different Do speak of "not needing the Japanese at this point," or "being better than the Japanese at . . . [insert your favorite art]." I can only shake my head. Competition of this sort has no place in the Do, as Westerners and Japanese should have the same goal: the understanding, dissemination, and preservation of traditional Japanese cultural arts and Ways. For when the Japanese aspects of an art are lost, so too are the art's history and character. In such an event, a different name should be applied to the art. At the least, if we alter the nature of such arts, we should note this by indicating that we teach or practice *American* karate or *European-style* ikebana, instead

Ki

Life energy, chi in Chinese, its meaning ranges in scope from one's spirit to the animating force behind the universe. See also ki-in.

Ki-in

Rhythm of life energy. Describes a sensitivity to and harmony with ki on all levels. When the artist senses and unites with the rhythm of the ki of nature, the essence of the universe is expressed in art. A sustained rhythmic flow of ki and attentiveness in the execution of a work results in the union of body and mind and the creation of artwork that resonates with a life-affirming rhythm and dynamism even centuries after its creation.

of trading off time-honored Japanese traditions. The Do are, after all, *Japanese* Ways, as evidenced by their Japanese names.

But is that all they are? Decidedly not. If they were, I wouldn't have bothered to write this book. Because, although I enjoy participating in parts of Japanese culture, that wasn't my original motivation for getting involved in the Do that I study. And it isn't why I continue to practice them. My original motives had much more to do with the universal aspects of the different Do, aspects whose understanding allow us to cultivate attributes that are valued regardless of cultural orientation. These aspects relate to the Way as much as to the Ways (for the Way is ultimately the Way of the universe).

The Ways are Japanese, and Westerners cannot divorce these arts or themselves from Japanese teachers or culture without losing something significant. Yet just as the Japanese Do are Japanese, they're also expressions of a Way that transcends nationalities and political boundaries. Understanding this universal Way has *nothing* to do with where we were born. It is the Way of humanity, the Way of the universe, and its significance is boundless and timeless.

So, while we Westerners perhaps can't understand the Ways as the Japanese do, we can certainly grasp *the Way* itself. And between Japanese and Western students of the Do, this is a most important link. Although I have heard a few Japanese sensei state that "only we Japanese can understand a Do," *none* of my fairly large number of Japanese friends, seniors, and teachers (of several different Do) has ever made such a proclamation because of the ease with which it can be misunderstood. If your sensei makes this assertion, what he is saying might be true, but only on one level, and perhaps not the most important one at that. Such a claim also indicates that the person espousing it is focused primarily on the particular, cultural aspects of the Do, and such a teacher is perhaps not the best one for a student interested in the meditative, universal attributes of the Way.

Because of my long exposure to the Japanese arts, Ways, and culture, several of my teachers have urged me to serve as a sort of bridge between East and West, particularly in terms of the Do. Other teachers in Japan espouse the international proliferation of the Ways as a vehicle toward *sekai heiwa,* or "world peace." Thus the Ways have at their core both universal and particular qualities. The particular manifestation of the Ways is Japanese, but they are also human expressions of the very heart of the universe.

Kokoro ugokeba shin tsukareru.
"When the mind is agitated, the spirit grows fatigued."
CHIEI

This is from Chiei's 1,000-character Sen-ji-mon, a classic work that points to a sentiment found in all the Japanese arts and Ways: spiritual stability stems from fudoshin—"the immovable mind." Yet like the painted characters above, fudoshin is calm and unwavering, but infinitely dynamic and capable of instantaneous action. Effective Japanese calligraphy mirrors this oneness of movement and stillness.

Chapter 3

THE SPIRIT OF
THE WAY

The general public and beginning students of the Japanese arts often think that art comes from the body. They assume that the hand determines the skillful brush work of the calligrapher or the arm the expert use of the sword. Those long immersed in these arts know, however, that it is the mind that paints through the hands, and the mind that cuts, even more than the sword. In short, the brush and sword cannot move unless they do so first in the mind.

Despite this truth, training in the Japanese cultural arts is often directed toward the body, and it takes a wise teacher to help us train the mind so it can lead the body to produce art. It's also important to study how to see the mind via the body and its artistic expressions. In this vein, Japanese calligraphers often speak of brush writing as being "a picture of the mind."

Art Emanates Directly from the Mind

The following simple experiment provides an idea of the importance of the mind in action. Place your hands about six inches away from each other, with the palms facing as shown in Figure 8. Sit or stand, keeping your body upright but relaxed, and focus your eyes gently on your hands. The aim here is to move your palms together by the sheer force of your concentration.

First, create a mental picture of your palms coming together. Second, simply think

FIG. 8. Stand with your hands six inches apart and bring them together with the force of your will. Keep your eyes focused on the hands.

that your palms are already together, and hold that thought. Third, "talk to yourself," mentally directing your palms to touch. Each of these directions represents essentially the same thought process, but some people have more success with one approach than another.

The point is to use the strength of a concentrated mind to influence the body and to see how your body responds automatically to whatever thought is in the mind.

An "automatic response" is key to this exercise, and the experiment is to see if it is attainable. Don't make any tentative assumptions. Avoid deliberately bringing the palms together. Rather, just focus resolutely on one of the above thoughts or images, sustain this state of concentration, and see what happens. If close attention doesn't waver, and the body remains relaxed, many find that the hands move without any intentional effort. This effortless feeling is unlike the way many of us move our bodies, and it is one of the secrets to arriving in art at maximum effectiveness with minimum strain.

Japanese Ways as a Reflection of the Mind

When asked exactly how a Do form functions as a Way, as opposed to simply a mechanical skill, I frequently explain that the body reflects the mind, and so any art can function as a visible representation of our spiritual condition. The movement of the body in dance or martial arts, the sound of the flute, the lines of ink on paper—all these actions equate to the mind expressing itself through the body, and as such, they offer opportunities to see more fully into our true nature. It is on this level that they function as Ways.*

It is also true that a Do is nothing more than mechanical action if the mind is misused. To further examine how the Japanese cultural arts can function as a depiction of the mind, we'll look at a variety of experiments like the one just presented. Since the mind controls the body, the vigor of our concentration will be the determining element in these exercises.

Harmonizing the Mind and Body

The creation of art requires inspiration, a knowledge of our tools, and an effective technique for using those tools. The skillful expression of ourselves in art (or life), with maximum efficiency

---

* The mind leads the body's actions, and this isn't limited to Japanese Do. Not long ago I read about pianist Liu Chi Kung. In 1958, he placed second to Van Cliburn in a Tchaikovsky piano contest. Not long after, during the Chinese Cultural Revolution, he was imprisoned. He lived alone in his cell for seven years. When he was released, he almost immediately played a series of highly acclaimed concerts. The public was amazed that none of his virtuosity had been lost, despite seven years without a piano. When asked how he had retained such a high level of skill with no piano to practice on, he replied, "I practiced every day in my mind."

Kodo

The Way of incense. Brought to Japan in the sixth century by Buddhist monks, who used the aromas in purification rites, incense became entertainment for aristocrats two hundred years later. During the fourteenth century, samurai would aromatize their helmets and armor with incense for an aura of invulnerability. In the seventeenth and eighteenth centuries, incense appreciation spread to the upper and middle classes. Kodo has long been a wellspring of spiritual sustenance in Japan. Modern practitioners use incense to heighten the ambiance of home or office, to delight guests, to honor special occasions, to calm the mind after a difficult day, and to comfort nerves before retiring.

and minimum effort, also requires the most effective ways of using the mind and body; our minds and bodies are, in the end, the sole tools we really own in life. Using the mind and body together naturally, practicably, and harmoniously allows for freedom of action and self-expression and is the most effective technique for using these tools. When the tie between mind and body is weak, novices in any art can observe a skill demonstrated by an instructor, or in a book, comprehend it intellectually, yet still fail to physically respond in the correct manner.

Comprehending the mind-body relationship, founders of the different Ways seem to have envisioned their arts in part as a means to directly discover how to coordinate these two most basic tools. By uniting the mind and body in a specific art, we have the chance to do so in daily living as well. It is in fact only when the mind and body work as a unit that we arrive at self-harmony. By learning to focus the entire coordinated energy of our minds and bodies toward a task, we also bring the force of our total being to bear upon that activity, thus discovering latent abilities and talents. In the Ways, this full and consolidated human power is sometimes referred to as ki.

Ki

Many Japanese arts and especially Ways mention ki as an important aspect of their teachings. In some arts, ki and its relationship to unity of mind and body are also explored. However, this exploration has commonly occurred on a largely intuitive level, involving years of experimental practice. The late Nakamura Tempu Sensei, founder of the Shin-shin-toitsu-do Japanese yoga system and a Western-style doctor, used his medical and scientific training to evolve a way of consciously and rationally studying ki and mind-body coordination. His teachings echo those of the creators of a number of Do, including calligraphy, flower arrangement, and martial arts.

Nakamura Sensei viewed the mind as an invisible aspect of the body and the body as a visible aspect of the mind. He equated the mind and body to a stream, with the mind the upper part and the body the lower. Unhelpful or negative elements that enter the upper part flow to the lower part and thus affect the body and our well-being. Understanding this effect, all the Ways value positive thought patterns.

The use of the word "ki" in this book may be different from what you have read elsewhere; it is a deliberate attempt to linguistically point at something that, owing to its holistic nature, is beyond description and yet still wholly tangible in everyday existence. Looking at ki from a different perspective will help show what I mean.

Physicists explain that every natural phenomenon is made up of variable mixtures of energy and matter. Such combinations constantly disintegrate into their component parts and reintegrate to create fresh phenomena. Matter can be transformed into energy, energy into matter. Neither can be annihilated absolutely. The entirety of all matter and energy has remained unchanging since our universe came into existence, and thus energy and matter—the essence of heaven and earth—are everlasting. From this viewpoint the innumerable parts of life that result from this aggregation of matter and energy are also infinite and eternal.

In recent years, a sort of union of quantum physics and deep

Kohai

One's junior in school, place of employment, or a traditional art. See also sempai; tate shakai.

mysticism has frequently been touted in popular media. Conversations with actual scientists and physicists reveal, however, that some of the claims are based on a poor understanding, and not all such views are embraced by the majority of scientists. Nonetheless, speaking broadly on the basis of the nature of energy and matter as outlined above, I use ki to indicate an indestructible union of matter and energy, something that is both ever changing and constant. Ki describes the elementary essence of existence, which experiences continual integration, disintegration, and re-creation. Ki can be understood as the connective tissue of creation, and, more specifically, as the component that joins mind and body. It is nondualistic in nature and thus beyond description, but it is not beyond experiencing.

It is also not exclusively spiritual or nonphysical. Ki is no more spiritual than it is material. It is, however, all encompassing. The body is ki as much as the mind is, in that every cell in the body exhibits a metabolic process, is alive, and thus has life energy. It is a visible form of ki, whereas the mind is refined, invisible ki. Ki is made tangible in nature through its manifestations, the limitless actions of nature's infinite number of integral parts. The action of ki is visible also in the body.

Because such verbalizing can easily become abstract, the late Dr. Nakamura invented straightforward exercises to experiment with the relationship between the mind and body, the intrinsic power of mind-body coordination, and the manifested action of ki. Since most Japanese arts, in addition to Shin-shin-toitsu-do, value the positive cultivation of ki and the harmony of body and mind, many top instructors in other arts and Ways have pursued Nakamura Sensei's teachings, and some of these concepts and exercises have found their way into other disciplines, notably the martial arts (aikido in particular) and healing arts.

This chapter presents experiments derived from Nakamura

Sensei's exercises for consciously experiencing ki and mind-body coordination. You'll need a friend to help with these experiments; since they aren't practiced alone, they amount to not only a means of studying the relationship between mind and body but also a method of examining interpersonal relationships.

EXPERIMENT ONE

Sit in a kneeling position, with your legs tucked under you and your left big toe resting on top of your right one. Leave some space between your knees and keep an erect posture. This is called *seiza*—"correct, calm sitting"—and it is utilized almost universally in some form in most Japanese cultural arts. If you cannot comfortably sit in this position, you can perform this exercise while seated in a chair.

With your shoulders relaxed and your elbows down at your side, place your palms together, fingers pointing up. Have your partner grip your wrists and try to pull your hands apart. Tensing your arms, resist your partner's efforts. If both of you are of roughly equal strength, your hands will separate quickly. This represents the limits of your body's power and exemplifies the way most people try to exert their strength and typically deal with conflict. But don't take my word for this. By experimenting and observing yourself and others in life, find out if this statement is true.

Next, visualize ki flowing through both arms and uniting at the palms and projecting upward from the fingertips. Try thinking of two powerful rivers that merge in your palms. To help create this feeling of merging, press your palms together firmly so that you experience a clear connection, but still lightly enough that tension isn't present. Ask your partner to attempt to pull your hands apart again, using the same amount of force as before (for

Koryu Bujutsu

Ancient martial arts. Refers to any of the classical martial arts used by Japan's feudal warriors.

FIG. 9. Seiza with palms together. Your partner tries to pull your palms apart. Visualize ki flowing toward the palms.

accurate comparison). Keep the palms gently pressed together as explained, but don't add extra muscular exertion. Do not resist, do not give up. Do nothing and simply sustain the image of ki flowing into your palms and merging, as shown in Figure 9. It might take several repetitions, trying both approaches each time, to thoroughly understand the ramifications of this exercise. (This will be equally true of the experiments that follow.) Once you get the hang of it, you should notice a tangible difference between the contrasting states of body tension/resistance and nonresistance with the correct use of ki.

Even if your muscles are strong enough to keep your partner from separating your palms on the first attempt, how does it feel when you do this? In comparison with the second approach, much more tension and effort are usually required to keep the hands together. The correct and natural use of ki isn't supernatural, but it does allow us to arrive at maximum efficiency with minimum effort, a quality valued in all the Ways and most prominently espoused by Kano Jigoro Sensei, the creator of judo.

EXPERIMENT TWO

Kneel or sit in a chair. Visualize the movement of ki toward your palms and ask your friend to try to pull your hands apart. They should be immovable as before. Then, while your partner continues to try to separate your palms, suddenly think of reversing the flow of ki, away from your palms and back into your body. In most cases, coinciding with this rapid pulling in of ki, the hands separate. Yet, your partner is simply maintaining the same pressure. What has changed isn't your friend's amount of force, and no contrast is being made in this case between muscular tension and the relaxed use of ki. Rather, the contrast lies in the way in which the mind is used and in the movement of ki itself.

When ki manifests in human form, it is analogous to a flame. When the flame burns cleanly and strongly, it gives off a powerful outward projection of heat. As the flame begins to die out, its radiation of heat withdraws. When the flame dies, its outward projection of heat also ceases.

Tension and/or the negative use of the mind in living is referred to in Japanese as *ki ga nukeru,* "withdrawal of ki," and it results in a loss of mind and body unification. When the body is relaxed and the mind positive, ki flows outward dynamically from all parts of the body, and mind-body coordination is sustained. Experiment Two compares these two conditions.

EXPERIMENT THREE

Remaining in the same position, have your friend press down on your fingertips, as shown in Figure 10. First, focus your attention on where your partner's palm is touching your fingertips, thus stopping your mind and ki at this point. Your body and arms are not tense, but not limp. Have your partner press down-

Ma

Literally "space" or "interval." Refers to the physical and/or psychological space that exists between people and/or things. It constitutes a technical principle in many of the Japanese arts and Ways. In the martial Ways, for example ma (or ma-ai) refers to a proper combative distance; in visual arts such as shodo, it describes the appropriate space between strokes of a character and between individual characters.

FIG. 10. Seiza with palms together. Your partner pushes down on your fingertips with his palm. Visualize ki flowing out of the fingers.

ward until your fingers buckle and/or your hands are forced down. How much power did it take to accomplish this action?

Now, keeping the same feeling in your body and arms, visualize ki flowing powerfully from your fingertips and up toward heaven. Aim for the sensation of it continuing forever to join with the infinite body of ki that is the universe, so that your flow of concentration remains unbroken. Once you obtain this feeling, have your partner press down on your fingertips as before, but this time don't stop ki at your friend's palm; imagine it passing through his or her palm, along with any other obstacles, and continuing infinitely. Even though your partner has used the same force as before, do you notice a difference in your personal power?

The positive use of ki requires not only a supple and calm posture but also a mind that doesn't become stuck on anything or at any point in time, as this serves only to stop the natural movement of ki. Life is constant change. The ki that animates the universe is likewise in constant motion. Living things are not static, and, as "living power," ki too is in continual motion—a movement that the Ways harmonize with rather than impede. This harmony with the ever-changing nature of existence is arrived at via nonattachment, a quality valued in all the Do. Exercise Three is the outward expression of nonattachment.

EXPERIMENT FOUR

Let's try something different. Seated as before, place your palms together. But this time, state aloud, in a strong and clear voice, "I cannot." Immediately following this, have your partner press down again on your fingertips. How much power does it take before your hands are forced downward?

Next, maintaining the same erect posture as before, with the identical feeling of being not tense and not limp, say aloud, "I can!" At this moment, your partner should apply downward pressure on your fingertips. Don't fight back, but don't give up. What happens?

Providing you believe what you're saying, a clear difference should be seen in your power in each case. The positive use of the mind, encouraged by positive verbal expressions, releases and enhances the movement of ki. Likewise, negative thoughts lead to psychological withdrawal, which parallels the withdrawal of ki in a negative state.

Although the mental imagery used in the preceding exercises can only be used consciously and at specific times in the Ways and in daily life, a positive mental state can be cultivated and sustained on an ongoing basis. This state, both positive and active, equals the dynamic outward movement of ki that exchanges with the ki of the universe. This movement and exchange of ki is infinite, eternal, and thus ultimately beyond description. Nevertheless, these exercises, because they help us to directly and personally experience something that can only be suggested, are valuable.

These exercises are not meant, however, to dazzle friends,

Misogi

Purification, a ritual associated with Shinto spiritual training. While saying prayers or chanting, devotees sometimes strip to loincloths and stand under a waterfall to cleanse the spirit.

overmystify ki, or lend to the Japanese arts and Ways an inscrutable occultism: the natural universe is miraculous just as it is, and people's failure to recognize this is the origin of much dissatisfaction in the world. The exercises demonstrate that using the mind and body as a unit is more effective than focusing exclusively on muscular power. What's more, the linked use of the mind and body increases the efficiency of muscular action. These experiments can also show by example how mind, body, and nature are interconnected, and how "reaching out" with ki to harmonize with nature can cause results that resonate in material realities (the body, in this example). The exercises give us an occasion to experience a different mode of dealing with the world, a way that is at once harmonious and effective.

The discovery of new and meaningful principles must, however, be complemented by their expression in everyday life for them to have worth. These experiments with ki offer insights that lead the way to examining how to use our bodies naturally, maintain a positive attitude, and focus our minds, which will bring benefits not only in the Ways but also in life in general. Without these insights, the experiments are little more than party tricks.

Once we see the benefits of a positive attitude, concentration, and a natural, relaxed posture, it's necessary to train the mind and body in a methodical, disciplined fashion in order to realize these characteristics. And the classical Japanese Ways offer an opportunity to train ourselves in precisely this fashion.

Hara

Like ki, the concept of hara has a long tradition in Japan and is a prominent aspect of many Ways. In Japan, and to some degree in other Asian countries, the focus of mental energy in the hara, or "abdomen," has been viewed as a means of realizing a person's complete potential. The Japanese view of the hara as a human's vital center is not unlike the Western notion of the heart or brain. Although there are differences between East and West relating to this subject, there are similarities that make it possible for Westerners to grasp the idea of hara. For instance, we speak of "having butterflies" in the stomach, and the Japanese expression *hara ga tatsu*, "the hara is rising up," means to be enraged; thus the notion of the hara as being a place of strong emotion is shared by both traditions. *Hara ga nai hito* refers to a timid person, "a person with no hara," which is comparable to our adage that someone "has no guts."

By now it has likely become clear that focusing the mind in the moment increases mental force and enhances the ability to coordinate mind and body, and, in the tradition of Japan's classical Ways, the place to concentrate on to achieve harmony of mind and body is the lower abdomen—the hara. There are compelling reasons for this idea.

The weight of the upper body reaches its maximum point of density beneath the navel, and this area corresponds to the center of gravity and balance for the body. If we focus the mind on the front surface of the lower abdomen, about four finger widths under the belly button, we're joining the mind and body in the same place and at the same time. Since the body dwells only in the present moment, by calming the mind in the hara, we're bringing our mind into the present as well. We've connected the mind and body.

In Japanese arts, ki is concentrated in the hara as a means of not just coordinating the mind and body but also bringing about mind-body stability and the restoration of composure. Calming the mind in the lower abdomen can aid in everything from accomplishing better balance in sports to stabilizing the mind before an

Mono no Aware

Aesthetic and spiritual concept describing a sentiment of pathos in response to an awareness of the fleeting nature of our relative world. Evokes a perception of beauty in the fragile, impermanent nature of life and suggests that genuine beauty depends on this very impermanence. Relates also to a harmoniousness with the constantly changing universe and with the universal cycles of creation and destruction.

FIG. 11. Seiza with palms together. Your partner sits next to you and pushes your chest with his fingertips. Focus your mind on the hara.

important phone call. To see the legitimacy of this statement, judgment based on actual practice is necessary; only through personal experience is it possible to learn what hara is and how it relates to life. Following, then, are additional exercises, relating to the hara.

EXPERIMENT FIVE

Sit in the same seiza position as before, with your palms together. Sit up straight, aligning your forehead with your lower abdomen. Have your partner sit at your side, facing roughly the same direction you are, and place his or her fingertips of one hand on your chest (Figure 11). Your partner then pushes against your chest using a steady, gradual pressure that is parallel to the ground. Focus your attention on the hand pushing you, and try hard not to tip over. It usually doesn't take much force under such circumstances to upset your balance—mental and physical.

Now, put your mind on as small a point as you can imagine about four finger widths below your navel. Have your partner apply the same amount of force as before as you allow the sensation of maintaining this natural center in the lower abdomen to continue. Again, neither give up nor fight back; just center yourself and do nothing. After you arrive at a centered feeling, don't force yourself to concentrate further. Just relax and let the feeling remain. What happens?

You can try the same experiment with pressure applied to the upper back, right between the shoulders. If the mind is calm and stable in the hara, the body will feel virtually immovable, which is a manifestation of fudoshin, "immovable mind," a concept I will come back to shortly. The state of mind indicated by this experiment is one that notices both external and internal phenomena but isn't upset by them. With this calmness of mind comes genuine relaxation, and when the above exercise is performed correctly, you'll feel a sense of deep relaxation under pressure. This relaxed state is vital for living a healthy, tension-free life. The exercise also points out the fallacy of the common idea of relaxation being comfortable but weak. Relaxation is actually our most powerful condition, but it must be properly understood for this power to be realized. And development of the hara can help us arrive at real and correct relaxation.

EXPERIMENT SIX

Assume the same position as before or sit in a chair, but this time let your lower back round and collapse. Sit heavily, resting your weight on your heels, using a posture that looks "small," as if it's collapsing in on itself (Figure 12). This amounts to a negative relaxation that is all too common. In fact, for many people this *is* relaxation. Ask your partner to push your chest as before. You'll probably find yourself unable to avoid tipping over—even if you concentrate the mind at the hara. In this posture, the weight of

FIG. 12. Seiza with palms together. Sit with your lower back rounded and slump. This is negative relaxation.

FIG. 12. Seiza with palms together. Sit with your lower back rounded and slump. This is negative relaxation.

your upper body doesn't settle below the navel and on the front surface of the hara; rather, it shifts up and back inside the body toward the lower back. Focusing the mind below the navel in such a case isn't effective since the center of balance is now somewhere else. Centralization in the hara is as physical as it is mental, and a state of collapse does not equal genuine relaxation.

Next, lower your buttocks gently and lightly onto your heels or a chair, adopting a position that both looks and feels expansive. Keeping the small of your back straight, open your chest naturally. While relaxing and dropping your shoulders, focus your mind four finger widths below the belly button and allow your upper body weight to follow the mind down to that point (Figure 13). Now when your partner applies the same force as before to your chest and back, the difference is remarkable. Real, positive relaxation is connected to calming the mind in the lower abdomen, but it also relates to the maintenance of a correct and natural carriage, thus the emphasis on an upright, dignified posture in many of the Ways.

Finding correct posture, deep relaxation, calm composure,

FIG. 13. Seiza with palms together. Sit with your lower back straight and with an expansive posture. This is positive relaxation.

and a more positive attitude, attributes needed for success in martial arts, healing arts, brush painting, and other Japanese Ways, is also important for living everyday life.

Ochitsuki

Ochitsuki, or "calmness," is universally valued in everything from tea ceremony to the game of go. Traditionally in the Ways, calmness of mind is often compared to a mirror: when the mind is still, it takes on the quality of a still pond, a mirrorlike condition that reflects life as it really is. And this mental composure has a physical expression.

Since the body reflects the mind, a stable body reveals a stable mind, and by the same token, a physical loss of balance indicates a mind that is not calm. The body is an object, albeit an animated object, and as such it is subject to certain natural laws—the law of gravity, for instance. Objects that are top-heavy are unstable. The currently popular Sport Utility Vehicles (SUV) are

SHIZUKA: *"Peaceful stillness." In the varied Japanese Ways, a still and peaceful state of mind is valued. When the mind is calm and immovable—even in the midst of physical activity—then the body relaxes and each body part settles naturally into its proper position. Most traditional Japanese art forms simultaneously unearth, cultivate, and express this condition of dynamic serenity.*

a good example of an object that is top-heavy and thus unstable, whereas the latest low-slung Porsche sports car exhibits a lower center of gravity and so greater stability. A mind that is calm induces the body to relax, allowing every body part to settle downward and into its proper and natural place. The hara is one such place, and settling down amounts to being more like the sports car than the SUV.

The following exercises will help demonstrate what this theory means.

EXPERIMENT SEVEN

Sit in seiza with the palms together. Lift the shoulders as shown in Figure 14. This amounts to drawing weight away from the hara and thus unsettling the body. Have your partner slowly lift your near elbow straight up toward the ceiling. Does it take much force to move it? Now, relax your shoulders and allow them to drop naturally. Have your friend lift the elbow again, using the same force as before (Figure 15). Which position is more stable?

Since the mind and body are one, instability in one represents instability in the other. If you go about your daily life with your shoulders raised, your mind likely reflects a similar state of agitation or unease.

EXPERIMENT EIGHT

Again in seiza with the palms together, have your friend sit

FIG. 14. Seiza with palms together. Lift your shoulders upward. Your partner can lit your elbow a couple inches with one hand because you are unsettled.

FIG. 15. Seiza with palms together. Keep your shoulders down. Your partner is unable to lift your elbow with one hand due to your settled weight.

next to you, facing the same direction as you. Focus your attention on the top of your head and relax into the posture previously described. Ask your partner to lift your near elbow straight up, using slow, steady pressure. Notice how little force it takes to move the elbow.

Then, visualize water dripping from your elbows and falling

Mu

*Buddhist concept refer-
ring to "the void" or
"nothingness," used in
the Do, which are con-
ceived of as particular
expressions of the Way
of the universe, to sug-
gest the indescribable
nature of the universe;
used also in compound
with other words to
describe different men-
tal states in the Ways.
See also mui.*

to the floor. While you sustain this image, relax and have your partner apply the same amount of power as before. In this case, the elbow should be much more difficult to lift. Why?

In the first instance, the upward movement of the mind caused a subtle unsettling effect in the body, making it more like the SUV. But in the second scenario, visualizing water falling downward created an internal settling of body weight that was more like the Porsche. Note that human beings jump—become unsettled—when they're surprised. And angry people often get red in the face owing to the upward movement of blood. Both examples point to the relationship between body and mind. Tension, unnaturalness of posture, lack of calmness—all these correlate to an upsetting effect on the body.

As we've seen, settling down isn't the same as sagging or collapsing. And locking the muscles, on the other hand, might keep the elbow down; but if your partner uses enough force, the entire body will tip over sideways. A relaxed (physical and mental) attitude is stronger than a tense one, and this relaxation comes from settling the posture. Calmness is dynamic, not dead.

These exercises bring an awareness of the effect of settling the body and concentrating the mind in the hara, and although some people might think that the cultivation of the hara involves always keeping the mind concentrated in the lower abdomen, common sense reveals that this is difficult to accomplish and unwise as an aim. I wouldn't want to ride in heavy traffic with someone whose mind was below the navel as opposed to on the road—even if they were driving a Porsche. The point of the previous experiments is to sense something beyond words, and to learn to identify when it is present and when it has been lost. Through ongoing training, the feeling of mind and body unity can be maintained as an unconscious habit.

I deliberately used the same posture for each experiment to

show how all these concepts are interrelated, and how each experiment ultimately produces the same feeling and result. It is that feeling that is important. It is beyond words, but not beyond our ability to experience. This experience is the essence of the Way.

Fudoshin

When real calmness arrives, the mind takes on an immovable characteristic known as fudoshin in many of Japan's Ways. Its physical expression is a posture that is so stable it may seem immovable as well—*fudotai*, the "unmoving body." (Review Experiment Five for an example of fudoshin/fudotai.)

Fudoshin doesn't mean a mind that *cannot* move, rather one undisturbed by the phenomena of the relative world, whether they are external or stem from the innermost recesses of the student of the Way. It's easy to misunderstand this point. Several years ago, I taught an elderly student named Charlie, who served in the American Navy during World War II. He was on a ship that had been bombed and was going down. Shortly after the initial explosion, the men rushed to abandon ship—all except one person, my student's friend, who was holding fast to a portion of the ship. Despite his shipmates' pleading, he was frozen like a statue, with a glassy-eyed expression. One of the sailors tried to pull him to safety, but he met with no success. Soon several men were pulling and tugging with all their might, but with no effect. In the end, Charlie was forced to bash this pillarlike sailor in the jaw, knocking him unconscious, before he could be moved. Charlie said to me, "That was some fudoshin, huh, Sensei?" Unfortunately, Charlie had confused being unable to move mentally, and therefore physically, with fudoshin. A deer frozen in the headlights of a car also exhibits this trancelike state, but it is not fudoshin.

Mui

Derived from the Chinese Taoist term wuwei. Refers to "doing nothing" and indicates a state of unaffected calmness in harmony with nature.

Arriving at mental and physical stability is altogether different. In this state, although the mind remains unperturbed by an emergency or traumatic situation, it is capable, because it is nonattached, of an instant reaction. Furthermore, although the body might be so settled and stable that it seems immovable, it is also capable of a quick reaction: the mind and body are calm and immovable when no need for action exists, and capable of immediate action when circumstances warrant a response.

This idea in turn ties to an old Asian maxim of the Ways: "motion in stillness, stillness in motion." When fudoshin is present, we are calm and physically stable even in motion, and at the same time, the mind is alert, aware, and intensely alive even in repose. Fudoshin describes a mind-body that is calm while in action, active while calm.

To acquire a real understanding of what this state is, actual experience is indispensable. And the Do provide situations in their practice that require fudoshin, thus giving us an opportunity to discover this quality for ourselves. Whether we're serving tea in chado or giving a demonstration of brush writing, we must concentrate. Yet if the mind becomes attached to one thought, we will be frozen like Charlie's buddy. Therefore, concentration, which makes possible effective functioning, is desirable, whereas attachment, which can lead to immobility, is not. Similarly, in odori or budo, our postures and movements must express calmness and stability, but they must also be capable of continuing motion. Since these arts require a psycho-physical state that is simultaneously immovable and capable of complete freedom of movement, there's less chance of misunderstanding the genuine nature of fudoshin than in an activity limited to seated meditation. Because the Do place us in situations requiring both immovableness and quick, flexible reaction, over a period of many years we also have many opportunities to discover the meaning of fudoshin.

Although the Ways embody meditative qualities, or at least a means for their realization, they are not akin to "stress management" classes that, in at least some instances, seek methods to eliminate or avoid stress. Getting rid of stress is not the point here. Death, after all, is a stress-free condition, and happy occasions like births and weddings are often stressful for the participants. So while the atmosphere in many Ways seems tranquil, it isn't a dead tranquillity; it's charged with ki. The tea ceremony, for instance, undeniably aims at a peaceful state, but ask any person who has seriously studied chado in Japan if their practice was without stress. You will likely hear about an exceptional moment or two, where despite some difficult situation or having made a massive mistake, they entered into a condition akin to being in the eye of a hurricane: complete stillness in the midst of adversity and activity.

SHIN: *This interpretation of the character shin is brushed in the formal kaisho script—equivalent to printing in English— and it means "true reality." Participation in one of the classical Do forms can help us wake up to the true nature of reality and discover unclouded perception.*

This stillness in the midst of action is different from the tranquillity pursued in other approaches. In college, I studied Hatha yoga under a wonderful teacher, from whom I learned a number of important things. We'd practice around lunchtime, and, being an exceptionally kind person, she went to lengths to create a peaceful sanctuary for us: dim light, burning candles, and the precursor to New Age music was playing in the background. During our concluding meditation, some students would even fall asleep. Most everyone enjoyed the practice, but a number of people mentioned that it was almost a shock to walk out into the brightly lit and noisy college hallways. More than one person wondered why, even after studying for some time, he or she was

Myo

A quality suggested by such words as "mysterious," "extraordinary," or "marvelous," it refers to a moment of realized perfection that is indescribable and that occurs within the process of—through the practice of a particular art—the embodiment of the Way.

unable to sustain the tranquillity experienced in this womblike environment for the rest of the school day. The problem was that, although the atmosphere was nonstressful, the orientation perhaps subtly encouraged an avoidance of stress as opposed to its transcendence.

There's nothing wrong with creating a peaceful environment to meditate in. The important point here is that the manner in which we approach practice determines what we get out of it, and what we do must relate to everyday realities. If meditation is a means of running away from stress or escaping from life, it's little different from a drug. Tranquillity is not a dead, negative relaxation, and it isn't the absence of stress. What exactly is it then?

The Japanese Ways involve relatively everyday activities, and their practice is therefore alive and often not stress free. The goal, however, isn't the elimination of stress; it is the transcendence of stress and the transformation of our perception of stress: fudoshin. With fudoshin as the objective, teachers often deliberately place students in stressful conditions to give them a chance to examine the nature of the immovable mind more fully. From the martial arts teacher's rapidly approaching punch to the shodo professor's admonition that touching up or redrawing is not allowed—no matter how absorbent the paper or how many people are watching—all the Do require an attitude that transforms stress from an enemy into an ally. It is an attitude of calm acceptance, a state of mind that views stress-filled situations not as moments to dread but as *opportunities* for self-knowledge, and such an attitude utterly transmutes the very concept of stress, giving rise to fudoshin.

Shisei

Just as the mind moves the body, our posture expresses our

mental state. When the mind is immovable, the body is exceedingly stable, and the posture appears natural and relaxed. *Shisei* describes this posture, but it also includes our mental carriage, which our physical state mirrors. Thus how we carry ourselves, physically and mentally, is of vital importance in many of the Do. Advanced sensei will frequently critique posture in painting, tea ceremony, Kabuki, or Noh drama. Perceptive students will realize this critique is also a comment on their mental state.

Because the Ways view the mind and body as one, their emphasis on posture is natural. Fudotai describes a body that is immovable. The bodily stability exhibited in the preceding experiments can be characterized as fudotai, an outward expression of the psychological stability that is fudoshin. Fudotai, like fudoshin, is a valued characteristic in the various Do (and isn't literally "immovable"; anyone's body can be displaced).

It is not necessarily the extent of immovability that is important; rather, fudotai is cultivated in relationship to fudoshin, and it is the fudoshin-fudotai connection that is truly valuable. This is true in martial arts, forms of Japanese dance, and other moving arts that require genuine balance in action.

The exercises introduced in this book are derived from the Japanese yoga of Nakamura Tempu Sensei, but since his death in the late 1960s they have been elaborated on and introduced into other Do by his top students like Tohei Koichi Sensei, Hirata Yoshihiko Sensei, and others. While not all teachers of the Ways will refer overtly to fudoshin and fudotai, or even to shisei (but will demonstrate these concepts in action), they are important in all of the Ways.

So let us briefly examine posture in the Do. Before proceeding, however, bear in mind that it isn't uncommon for interpretations of correct posture to vary between teachers and arts. Nonetheless, certain common points can be found, and although

Netsuke

Netsuke date back to the seventeenth century and are still carved as a craft today. Netsuke served both practical and artistic purposes. They were used when wearing a kimono to secure purses and were frequently used to hold tobacco pouches. See also inro.

the following explanation might not match what everyone is doing in the Ways, it can serve as a useful starting point.

In general, all the Do aim for unity with nature and strive to manifest naturalness. This naturalness is often characterized as *shizentai*, or "natural posture." It does not necessarily refer to a specific stance (although it can) but points more toward a physical carriage that is natural and harmonious. Such a posture is in harmony with itself and nature: whether in repose or in motion, every part of the body functions to support every other part of the body. In particular, the hara, as the midsection of the body, unifies the action of the upper and lower halves of the body, which, in order to effect harmony, must work together.

In Western sports, for example, a baseball player rotates his waist as he swings the bat. To bat predominantly with the arms would diminish power by producing a disconnected movement and posture. Similarly, when a bowler steps forward to release the ball, she shifts her hara in the direction of the pins as she releases the ball. In both examples, the action of the hara allows the athlete to unite the force of the upper and lower halves of the body, bringing the force of the entire body into play. We've seen how focusing mental strength in the lower abdomen leads to a unification of mind and body, and since the body follows the mind, this focusing can also encourage us to move from the hara, as in these two examples.

In Experiment Six, we examined posture and its relationship to the hara. A brief review of the exercise might enhance your understanding of the discussion of shisei that follows. In particular, the illustrations are a valuable guide to a correct posture for the Japanese arts and Ways and to its usefulness in daily life for gaining better health, balance, coordination, and composure.

A natural, stable posture is relaxed, upright, and aligned. This posture is essential in everyday living, and it must be maintained in the Do. In the illustrations of people sitting in seiza, notice that they sit lightly on the heels, with the big toes crossed and some space between the knees. Although seiza is difficult, at first, for some people to adopt, it is effective for centering weight forward and down into the hara. Think of this point as a natural center in the lower abdomen that corresponds to your center of balance and gravity. When sitting in seiza or in a chair, sit lightly, almost as if your "bottom" were sore, and maintain a relaxed posture that looks "big." Avoid sagging. When standing or walking, it is important not to slump or raise the shoulders, or rest flat and heavily on your heels.

Many times during meditation or in practicing the Ways, and even in daily life, there is a tendency for the head to sag forward, while the neck collapses and bends, producing a "hump" at its base. The rest of the spine soon curves in on itself as well. You can correct this by concentrating on the hara and moving your head. Mentally release your muscles (along the neck and spine in particular). Visualizing your hara as a sort of anchor, direct the top of your head up and away from your hara, and then draw in your chin and bring your forehead back into alignment with your lower abdomen. Allow the spine and neck to lengthen until your posture is aligned. Envisioning the muscles along the spine growing longer and wider is an effective technique to bring this about. If you concentrate deeply and relax, the body will move naturally into the correct position. On the other hand, be careful not to force your body into an overly erect posture. By relaxing and using visualization, expand the chest and broaden the back and shoulders. The ears, shoulders, and pelvis should be squared and parallel to the floor.

In practicing sumi-e or shodo, students often sit in a chair, particularly in the West. If you sit in a chair, avoid sitting with your legs outstretched, as this causes your pelvis to roll backward and your lumbar region to curve outward in a slump. Sit with your feet

Nippon-to

The Japanese sword, popular symbol of the spirit of Japan and the soul of the samurai. Prized by fanciers worldwide, the Japanese sword is a tangible expression of Japanese history, customs, and aesthetics. From its appearance, aficionados can discern the contemporary style of combat, the tradition in which the smith worked, the aesthetic principles of its period, as well as the historical evolution of sword making in Japan.

Niwa

A Japanese-style garden that aims at symbolizing a vast natural panorama in a limited area. Influenced by Zen and Shinto traditions, the niwa effects a naturalistic, asymmetrical beauty arrived at through a harmony of spatial arrangement.

flat on the floor or tucked under the chair (almost as your legs tuck under your hips in seiza). This maintains your natural lumbar curve and shifts your weight toward the front surface of the lower abdomen, exactly where you want to center your weight and mind.

Regardless of the art being practiced or the particular position being used, relax your face and eyes and find the most comfortable posture within the context of the above instructions. This act of centering produces a particularly steady position. To sustain this free and relaxed condition of stability, avoid leaning in an unbalanced way, as the weight of the upper body must be in equilibrium at the hara.

The correct shisei is a posture that is unified, mind and body working together, upper and lower sections of the body aligned, and every body part working with every other part. This is the posture of unification, and it can be as beneficial in daily activities as it is in the Ways.

Do Chu no Sei and Hyoshi

Although we use the word "posture" to describe shisei, in the Ways posture is rarely static. Whether we practice tea ceremony, dance, or *raku* pottery, movement is involved. Thus, in the Ways of Japan, we experience shisei as a series of linked postures that form the essence of movement.

This emphasis on movement in the Do isn't surprising: the Ways have as their objective discovering the Way of the universe in the midst of activity. Do forms are, in fact, everyday actions—writing with a brush, preparing tea, arranging flowers—that have been "spiritualized" to become meditative disciplines. Although some Ways use seated meditation, the basic nature of meditation in the Do is dynamic, that is, "moving meditation."

For most of us, our lives are marked by activity, visual stimu-lation, and noise; we do not sit perfectly still with our eyes closed in silence. And yet sitting alone and perfectly still in a quiet, dimly lit room is precisely the sort of meditation many people engage in. That this form of meditation doesn't reflect what we do in our lives might explain the difficulty in transferring the meditative state into daily life.

It is indeed easier to unite mind and body while in repose; it is harder to sustain psycho-physical harmony in motion, and even more challenging to sustain this state of unification in relationship to others. Since many Ways involve activity, often in relationship to others (in the case of arts such as budo, chado, odori, music, and similar Ways), and because they're usually performed with the eyes open, they are practices of dynamic meditation that relate closely to life. They are also practices that can help us to translate the benefits of seated meditation into daily activity.

This quality of Do forms, active meditation, is pointed to in the phrase *do chu no sei* (sei, "calmness"; chu, "during"; and do, "movement"), which can be translated as "stillness in motion" or "calmness in the midst of action."

Another important term in relation to movement in the Ways is *byoshi*. Hyoshi describes "timing" and "rhythm." In budo timing is critical. In jujutsu and aiki-jujutsu, there is a technique called *aiki nage*. Aiki—ai, "harmony," and ki, "life energy"—describes harmony with the life energy of the opponent and the universe; *nage* means "throw." (The term *kokyu nage*, "breath throw," is used by some aikido practitioners to describe this or similar techniques.) In one version of this technique, an attacker attempts to seize your wrist with both hands (Figure 16).

Moving the opponent into an unbalanced condition, which always precedes a throw, can be difficult once your wrist has been grasped, but beginners nevertheless attempt to struggle against the

FIG. 16. The attacker's objective is to hold the opponent's wrist with two hands. (Figs. 16–20 illustrate the concept of hyoshi, or timing and rhythm, in Japanese arts, using jujutsu as an example.)

FIG. 17. The attacker is about to hold the opponent's wrist with two hands. He is leaning slightly and his hands are a couple of inches from the opponent's wrist. This is when the opponent should start to move—before he is held.

often superior physical strength and body weight of the other person. And although an individual might have a heavy body, there is no such thing as a heavy mind.

In budo, as in all the Ways, the mind moves the body, and the body's responses mirror the mind. Therefore, if you can draw

FIG. 18. The opponent has dropped his bent wrist to a point near his leg, leading the attacker into an unbalanced position. The attacker is unbalanced and holding the opponent's wrist with two hands at this point.

the attacker's mind in an advantageous direction, his body will follow.

The way to achieve this is to simply let your arm fall to your side when the opponent is just about to touch your wrist, rather than waiting until your wrist is already in your opponent's grip (Figure 17). Dropping the arm too soon will only cause an alert assailant to stop or pull back; too late, and your wrist is trapped and you are left to struggle against the entire weight and strength of the opponent's body. But if you move at the last second, smoothly and calmly, the attacker will follow the dropping arm into an unbalanced condition (Figure 18).

This just-so timing is what hyoshi refers to: at just the right moment, lead the opponent to believe your wrist is going to be where he expects, and then move it at the last second, but smoothly enough so that the attacker believes if he just reaches a little bit farther . . . he'll be able to grab it. He will, but in an unbalanced way. And he will not want to stay off balance for long. Anticipating his desire to rise, add power to his upward thrust, stay just a bit ahead, and lead the opponent upward with both arms (Figure

FIG. 19. The opponent turns and leads the attacker upward with both arms.

19). This causes his weight to be unsettled, since your added power was unexpected, and the attacker's body "pops up" suddenly as a result. Next, because of this unsettling action, his weight will fall back down and onto the back of your wrist. At the moment the weight descends, drop your wrist and other arm out from under the attacker; the effect will be like pulling a chair out from under someone. A fairly spectacular fall is the result (Figure 20; the arms continue to drop further downward than can be seen here). All of this is accomplished through rhythm and timing.

The first action is dropping the arm and letting it swing back up. In relation to rhythm, this can be considered one beat. Next, you drop both arms for the throw, and that's the second beat. It should take no more than two seconds to complete this version of aiki nage, but novices often break the rhythm by creating three beats instead of two. That is, they drop the attacked wrist—hesitate—then raise both arms, and third, drop the arms again to throw.

But the throw isn't accomplished because the hyoshi was wrong. The first beat is down/up, not down and up. This sudden down/up action makes advantageous use of the opponent's psy-

FIG. 20. The opponent drops his arms and throws the attacker with *aiki nage.*

cho-physical reactions. A break in rhythm only inhibits those reactions. Hyoshi is critical.

Timing and rhythm are also important in the other Ways. Let's take a look at the visible rhythm in shodo.

Japanese characters, although sitting motionless on the paper, should nevertheless look like they're moving. This is an example of motion in stillness in shodo, an art that displays a visible rhythm in the manner that music evidences an audible rhythm. Such a rhythm can be achieved in shodo, and in other Ways like budo and chado, only by means of profound relaxation. Relaxation allows us to achieve calmness in action and action in calmness. Moreover, we're able to find and maintain rhythm only when we stay calm despite outward movement. Do chu no sei and hyoshi are interrelated, and they are essential for not impeding the flow of ki, and in turn the dynamic flow of the brush itself.

Relaxation is vital. Relaxation comes, however, only with naturalness. If we feel tension in any part of the body, or during any brush movement, it is necessary to find the source of the

Noh

The oldest form of Japanese theater, a dance-drama centering around heroic themes relating to gods, humans, madness, and demons and featuring a chorus of musicians and singers, masked principal actors, and highly stylized movement, costuming, and scenery.

unnaturalness in our posture or way of moving. For example, the movement might be overextended, or we might be cramped by poor posture. A straightforward way to tell if a position or action is truly relaxed and natural is to pause at different points during the painting. Hold the position for thirty seconds and notice if you can "feel" the muscles in some part of your body. If there is a strong muscular sensation, it usually indicates the presence of tension.

No muscular sensation reveals that the muscles are properly relaxed and that the posture and movements are natural. We are unconscious of our bodies and selves, in a state, not of numbness or unawareness, but of serenity. This condition is the forgetting of self that occurs at a moment of peak performance in any activity, when we are aware of only the instant and the action of that instant. This is referred to as *muga ichi-nen*, or "no self, one thought." It is this state that allows shodo to transcend mere skillful brush writing.

In shodo, the brush is moved according to a definite rhythm. Rhythm both demonstrates and promotes coordination. All arts, including shodo, have a unique rhythm. Each character likewise has a particular cadence with which it is painted. Excellence results from finding and maintaining the correct rhythm. Breaks in rhythm register breaks in coordination of body and mind, and they usually happen when the flow of ki is broken during a lapse in mindfulness or a moment of tension.

Every character has a fixed number of strokes that must be brushed in a strictly defined order. The brush moves smoothly from one stroke to the next, flowing in an unconstrained and easy manner within each character. As the stream of life energy flows in a stable rhythm from one character to the next and from one line of characters to the next, a dynamic and yet balanced feeling results, and this lends the entire composition an appearance of unified rhythm.

To facilitate an unbroken rhythm and flow of ki, novices can count out loud as they make each brush stroke. Count each stroke like a beat in music, allowing about one second per beat. This is a simple way to get the feeling of unbroken rhythm in shodo. As students progress, they discover that the rhythm between (and during) certain strokes speeds up, and at other times slows down. Like a river, the fast and slow movements in shodo do not represent a break in rhythm so much as natural expressions of variation in a single, unified flow.

Every part of life has its own rhythm that must be found to be successful in a given activity. Sustaining rhythm also allows us to relax within what it is we're doing. Going against natural rhythm, in our work or personal relationships, only creates conflict. Nature has its own rhythm. To discover that rhythm, through any of the Japanese arts and Ways, is a fascinating, never-ending pursuit.

Ochitsuki

State of calmness universally valued in everything from tea ceremony to the game of go.

Kan

While the Ways consist of movements and trained techniques, the training method is based around *kan*. And when we become proficient in a Way, our movements and techniques are born of kan. Yet kan itself is elusive.

Kan can be translated as "intuitive perception," but the concept also includes the idea of "quickened insight"; it is the ability to perceive what is about to take place even before, for example, all the action has played out. In the Ways, kan refers to learning through direct experience, personal discovery, and intuition, and by means of the cultivation of heightened intuitive perception itself.

The cultivation of kan in a Do depends on the student's approach to its study and practice. As I've stressed, reading about

Odori

Style of dance usually associated with Kabuki drama but also practiced as an art in its own right. Mai is a dance form allied with Noh theater. These two forms, along with folk dancing, comprise the three main types of Japanese dance.

certain principles can be useful, but only through direct, actual experience does understanding occur. Effective teaching in the Do is like pointing a finger toward a desired end, and skilled teachers of a Do try to find the best methods of pointing students in the right direction, but in the end it is up to the student to see where the finger is pointing and travel the revealed path.

The Ways involve activity, and so their underlying principles can be discovered only by doing. This means hundreds or thousands of repetitions of basic exercises and techniques. Through such repeated practice—practice engaged in with full consciousness and not just mechanical repetition—beginners *feel* the principles their teacher has pointed to. It's important to keep in mind that a teacher points students toward an intuitive (as much as intellectual) understanding of a principle. Thus a shodo teacher will hold a student's hand from above so that the student can sense stroke pressure and rhythm, and the same shodo teacher, in response to a question about a character, will, rather than just verbally explaining the answer, repeatedly paint the character as the student observes. In budo, the martial arts teacher will "explain" an important throwing technique by repeatedly throwing the student using that specific technique, and the same budo sensei will allow himself to be thrown repeatedly to determine the effectiveness of the student's skills.

In teaching a variety of Ways for a number of years, it has been my experience that Americans, for example, often want to know what an art is all about without actually trying the art they're interested in. Certainly there are exceptions, but I've encountered many people who would like me to tell them what a given Way is, how it is practiced, and what the practice is like—all without actually stepping through the door of our dojo. Such an approach significantly limits what can be explained and certainly what can be understood of a Way.

By virtue of mindful repetition and practice, the pupil of a Way begins to intuitively feel the underlying, connecting principles, called *gensoku*, that the instructor has made reference to. Over a period of years these gensoku are internalized. Again, this takes place not by means of mere thought, but by sensing and doing, over and over again.

KAN: "Intuitive perception." Brushed in the semicursive style of the renowned Chinese calligrapher Ogishi.

Once this process of embodying the gensoku takes hold, the novice disappears, and a real disciple of the Way emerges, a disciple who is able to vary and alter the fundamental techniques and forms of her art without violating the art's gensoku. In short, the disciple can now create *henka*, or personal variations, based on internalized principles.

In the course of a disciple's progress, he or she may reach a point in flower arrangement, for example, where flowers seem to arrange themselves. In budo, he may start to spontaneously create entirely new techniques appropriate to the combative situation of the moment, while the shodo expert might, in response to a particular condition or event, intuitively alter a character in mid-brush stroke, only to create something more beautiful than intended. And so, we return to kan: an immediate perception of what is needed that is also invariably right but rarely prearranged.

Additionally, because in the Ways teachers instruct by example and demonstration as much as by direct explanation, and students learn by doing what they've been shown, longtime students develop a profound sensitivity to their teacher. This enhanced sensitivity to the ki of others is also an expression of kan.

Okuden

From oku, "inner," and den, "teachings," refers to the hidden or secret aspects of an art or its school. Used in conjunction with shoden *(beginning) and* chuden *(intermediate) levels of instruction or competence, it indicates the advanced stages.*

In any activity performed with other people, and certainly in Japanese music, dance, and the martial arts, sensitivity to the ki of others is necessary to sustain harmony. A musician who waits to hear what the others are playing will fall behind the beat. A dancer who hesitates to observe the other dancers has lost the rhythm. And in the martial arts, if you wait to see what kind of attack is being launched, by the time you figure it out, you've already been grabbed or hit. Still, a misjudgment can lead the musician to play the wrong note, the dancer to step at the wrong moment, and the martial artist to anticipate the wrong attack. The way out of these sorts of difficulties is, more than by use of the intellect, the development of kan. And, not surprisingly, direct, personal experience—*doing*—is needed to know kan.

Following is an exercise that will help you directly discover the nature of kan.

EXPERIMENT NINE

As with the previous exercises, you'll need a friend to help you with this. Either stand or sit in seiza and extend one arm in front of you with the palm up. Your partner lays his or her palm on top of yours (Figure 21), and your friend then begins to slowly move his or her hand up, down, sideways—in any direction. Your job is to stick to your partner's hand. The palms shouldn't separate, nor should you feel any collision between the two hands if, for example, your friend suddenly lowers his or her palm. The goal is harmony.

Reaching and sustaining such harmony can be difficult, particularly as the exercise progresses. Next, close your eyes gently, without creating tension. Your friend continues to move his or her hand, and now more than ever, you must truly *sense* where to follow. A still more challenging exercise is to extend both palms

FIG. 21. An illustration of kan, or intuition. Stand with your palm touching your partner's palm. Your partner's palm is on top of your palm. Sense and follow the movement of your partner's hand and ki.

upward, eyes closed, and ask your partner to move both his or her hands simultaneously in any direction. Finally, he or she should move both hands quickly, then slowly, and with sudden stops—all without your palms separating or clashing.

This is a fun albeit formidable test of sensitivity to others and the ability to sustain harmony. The key to discovering harmony in action in this exercise, and in living, is kan. More concretely, waiting to see where your partner's hand goes or attempting to guess its course will most often be ineffective—but there is a solution to this exercise.

Before your partner moves, his or her mind (and thus ki) will flow in that direction first. For instance, if I'm going to pick up a glass, first I have the intention to do so, then my ki moves toward the glass, and finally the observable action occurs. The same can be said for any movement in life. The body doesn't move, act, or speak by itself, without mental activity.

If we calm the mind, we can pick up many subtle events taking place in our environment, including the movement of ki in the universe. By intuitively sensing where ki is going before the hand itself moves, and by acting as soon as we perceive this movement rather than waiting until we've seen the hand actually move, we can match our friend's actions. But this kind of sensitivity requires real calmness more than deliberately trying to sense something or attempting to read your partner's mind.

Frequently, students will think too much to arrive at kan. Deliberately thinking about where your friend's ki may or may not be going rarely works. Rather, notice what goes through your mind when you open a door or turn a page of this book. Obviously you have the intent to perform a particular action, but this intent is so quick as to be imperceptible under most circumstances, and the same can be said for the motion of ki preceding your partner's hand movement: by the time you finish trying to feel his or her movement of ki, the action has occurred.

The key is to calm the mind, and do nothing. Move only when you feel like moving. If the mind is truly calm, your feelings will accurately reflect where your friend's hand is about to go. Genuine calmness is the crucial ingredient in kan, along with repeated practice of activities that lead to the needed sensitivity. Calmness can be arrived at in a variety of ways, but a time-honored approach in the Japanese Do involves stilling the mind at a single spot below the navel. Still the mind as described in what follows and try the exercise again and compare the results of both attempts.

Sit or stand lightly, displaying an erect but relaxed posture that appears expansive and allows the body's weight and center of gravity to settle at a point in the lower abdomen. Allow the mind to focus on the natural center below the navel; in other words, focus the mind in the same spot where the weight has settled, which corresponds to your center of balance. Drop and relax the shoulders and upper body, as if dropping your weight into the low- er abdomen, but without slumping or going limp. Once this calm, centered feeling has been attained, extend your upturned palm or palms, and perform the exercise as before, except this time simply move when you feel you should. The sensing of ki takes place naturally in this state of refined relaxation and composure.

A calm, composed mind can be compared to a perfectly still body of water. In this state, even the slightest breeze registers on the water's surface. If, on the other hand, the water is already turbulent, it takes a lot of wind before any change is noticeable on its surface.

Thus, when we calm the mind, even subtle changes in our environment register rapidly, including changes in the movement of ki, but if the mind is agitated, we fail to notice all but the biggest changes taking place around us, making our reactions slow or nonexistent. Notice that the water doesn't try to feel the breeze. Because its surface is calm, it responds naturally, and we can learn to do the same in this exercise and in our lives. Japanese arts and Ways give us a chance to study this in a structured environment.

We have to distinguish between the sensitivity mentioned here and the often spurious occult-type practices touted in some quarters. Certainly sensitivity to ki is involved in kan, but ki is all encompassing, as physical as it is mental. The mind and body are one, and the Ways are based on this fact. So, in Experiment Nine, we're not aiming at a psychic sixth sense that is separate from our physical senses of touch, hearing, and so on. To do so would simply engender a separation of mind and body, making sensitive and harmonious action impossible. Ki is everywhere and everything. Kan, in the Ways and in everyday life, requires a natural, holistic sensitivity to all aspects of ki, both physical and mental, visible and invisible.

Omote

Front or outside. Refers to what is visible, and in the context of human relations, relates to a "public face." With its counterpart, ura ("back," "inside," "hidden"), it speaks of a dualism in the arts of Japan and the visible-invisible, in-yo nature of the universe. See also ura.

Ryu and Den

The Ways contain some concepts—kan, for example—that are relatively elusive and perhaps prone to diminishment or misunderstanding over the course of time. *Ryu* were developed to help preserve and pass down types of knowledge and related techniques. But before I discuss ryu directly, it might be useful to talk first about water.

Japanese culture has a long association with water. Of course the Japanese islands are surrounded by the sea, and fishing and the sea's bounty have always had a central place in Japanese life. Further, owing to Shintoism, the Japanese have a long connection with water in a spiritual sense. Shinto emphasizes purity, both of body and of spirit. "Ritual purification," or misogi, is a primary aspect of Shinto. Owing partly to Shinto's emphasis on cleanliness and partly to Japan's connection with the sea, many forms of misogi involve meditation under waterfalls, bathing in the ocean, and purification in icy rivers. And it isn't uncommon for these water-based austerities to take place in the dead of winter—a surefire way to drive just about any impurity out of you!

Thus, for geographical, historical, and religious reasons, aspects of Japanese consciousness are permeated with the element of water, and so are the Ways. And now we come to ryu. Ryu is a word relating to flow or currents in water. It is also used to describe the idea of transmitting inspiration and techniques from a Way's founder to succeeding generations. The same word also denotes a specific style, tradition, and system of art. Practitioners of classical martial arts will identify themselves as students of, for example, Tenshin Shoden Katori Shinto Ryu, or of Hontai Yoshin Ryu. A practitioner of flower arrangement might speak of being associated with Ohara Ryu, while another teaches Sogetsu Ryu.

Early in the development of the Japanese arts, trial and error revealed the best techniques in, for example, making pottery, wielding a sword, and manipulating a brush. In order to avoid reinventing the wheel, at some point in this ancient development, calligraphers, martial artists, flower arrangers, and others started to keep track of what worked. Frequently more than one approach would create a similar result, and different traditions of practice were thus born.

RYU: *Brushed in the antique gyosho script of the celebrated calligrapher Ogishi, ryu refers to a handed-down system of techniques. More than a mere style of a particular art form, a ryu is an unbroken living tradition that flows through the ages complete with multiple generations of head teachers and students. Practitioners of the various Ways often indicate that they are members of a particular ryu of flower arrangement, calligraphy, or other arts.*

For geographical and historical reasons, contact between people and places within Japan was limited, and this, too, encouraged the development of distinctive versions of the same art or Way in different parts of the country. Another important factor in the emergence of ryu is the heritage of ancestor veneration in Japan. If, for example, a person living long ago in the Aizu fiefdom (on the island of Honshu) originated, recorded, and taught a particularly effective version of a martial art, it would distincly differ from the same martial art as practiced in a different fiefdom located on the southern island of Kyushu. To emphasize its uniqueness, the leader of the particular fiefdom and/or the founder of the art would give it a name expressing its uniqueness. What is more, the founders of such ryu sometimes claimed to have received the teachings through a divine revelation, or, if not, they were revered as especially wise individuals. Combine this exalted view of the founder with students steeped in the veneration of ancestors, and you have fertile cultural ground for reverence of a founder, whose creation becomes a living entity passed from generation to generation. Such entities are called ryu and are widespread in all the Japanese arts and Ways.

Origami

"Paper folding." The art ranks with painting and sculpture and is associated with stylized traditions such as ceremonial etiquette and paper adornments attached to presents (noshi). In previous eras, paper was too costly to use for a hobby, so origami was resolutely established and restricted to ceremonial events. The oldest cases are male and female paper butterflies employed to adorn sake cups at marriage rituals.

Regarding the development of ryu, Dave Lowry writes in *Michi Online:*

> Partly because the mass production of literature is a historically recent development in Japan, and partly because a transmission of the Ways was considered to be too intricate and intimate to depend upon a textbook approach, the Ways were carefully codified and passed along personally from master to disciple. Eventually, this individualized method encouraged the formation of separate schools, or ryu, each with its own distinctive curriculum. A good example is found in kado, the Way of flower arranging. To the neophyte, two arrangements from the Ikenobo and Ohara schools of kado might seem quite similar. To the master, however, each is markedly different, reflective of the particular style of the school from which its creator came. The individual ryu also propagated their own preciously guarded "secret" techniques, which further serve to distinguish them. As with flower arranging, the secret itself might be as minor as a particular way of cutting flowers to retain their freshness longer. In the varying ryu of kendo, the Way of swordsmanship, the secrets often entail special tricks of body movement in attacking an opponent or luring him into a vulnerable position. Today, whether it be fencing or flower arranging, schools of the Ways are maintained by a continuum of headmasters and their loyal followers, each with its own teachings and traditions.[12]

That the ryu are living traditions means that a ryu ceases to exist when its exponents die out or when the skill level of its practitioners is lost. More than a collection of technical knowledge, a ryu truly is a living being that exists within the collective mind and body of its practitioners. As traditions that are alive, they cannot be maintained through only the written or spoken word but must *flow like water* from disciple to disciple, each of whom must feel and discover for him- or herself a particular tradition's true meaning.

In shodo, for example, it's common for the sensei to grasp the student's hand and literally paint using the pupil's limb and brush as an extension of the teacher. (Speaking as a teacher of calligraphy, this is much easier said than done!) When I studied a ryu of Japanese bodywork, my teacher would treat me and then have another student apply the same treatment to me. My job was to let my fellow student know if the treatment felt the same and, if not, identify how it differed from the sensei's. Then, my fellow student and I would switch roles. In other cases, my sensei would treat me and then have me apply the same treatment to him, again comparing the feeling of the therapy, the movement of ki, and the precise location of pressure. In this way, the quality and aliveness of the ryu are sustained and passed on.

I also mentioned *den* at the beginning of this section. Den means "transmission," a transmission that is essentially beyond words and one that lies at the heart of the ryu. Nevertheless, some ryu of tea ceremony, flower arrangement, and other arts have written records of their teachings that are handed down from generation to generation of the ryu's leaders and disciples. These recorded teachings, or *densho*, are often difficult to decipher for all but those immersed in the ryu, who have received the transmission "from mind to mind." Den can also refer to a particular tradition or teaching, and can thus have a meaning similar to ryu. For instance, teachings that are orally transmitted are called *kuden*, and esoteric traditions and methods are referred to as *hiden*. Although kuden and hiden can sometimes be found in books, their actual meaning can be discovered only through practice, a convention firmly anchored in the flow of generations of teachers and disciples.

Transmission of a ryu takes place in an intimate manner, and indeed it wasn't uncommon historically for teachers to have *uchi deshi*, live-in apprentices, who not only received formal lessons in a Way but also cared for the sensei by attending to household chores and other duties. With certain teachers, this tradition has continued unaltered into the twenty-first century.

The practice fulfilled, and fulfills, very real needs: immersion and intimacy. While I have never lived with any of my teachers, I have spent a fair amount of time with some of them outside the classroom or dojo setting. In some cases, I've served as an *otomo* for certain sensei. An otomo does everything from assisting with classes to carrying a teacher's luggage and making tea, and besides learning a great deal from the increased, intensified, and in-depth training such closeness afforded, I was surprised to discover that I also learned significant lessons from waking the sensei up in the morning and preparing the bath.

Such learning is not, however, unexpected when you realize that the arts and Ways are not only art forms but also Ways of living. By being close to a teacher, we have an opportunity to see the Way in action, to more directly experience what we are studying as a genuine Way of life. In one case, this took the form of my noticing how Kobara Ranseki Sensei, the headmaster of my ryu of calligraphy and painting, still practiced every day, even after over fifty years of training. Each morning he would rise at five and, after prayer, begin his practice. At the age of seventy, Kobara Sensei fell ill and was unable teach formal shodo classes for some time. Yet I understood that Sensei was still teaching a Way, and I stayed in touch with him during this period, noticing that he continued to practice despite his life-threatening illness. He told me that he had barely enough strength to lift a glass of water, but "the brush isn't that heavy, so I'd still like to practice." And he did practice, almost every day.

To some, this has little to do with painting, and this might be true in a narrow sense. But it has everything to do with the Way of calligraphy and the soul of Kobara Sensei's ryu. Sensei, his artwork, and his ryu all embody the same quiet, indomitable spirit.

Although living with a teacher might not be possible, it is important to attend classes and spend time with a teacher to the greatest extent possible; by doing so, you will understand that the Way transcends the techniques of a given art.

Seishin Tanren

Participation in a ryu represents a serious commitment since it is not aimed primarily at the acquisition of technical abilities, for example how to paint or how to arrange flowers. Knowledge of techniques can be handed down, but arriving at real skill in these techniques, no matter how effective the instruction, remains always an intensely personal matter. Despite slick sales pitches, encountered sometimes in Japan as well as in the West, no individual can simply *give* you skill. You must *find* it yourself.

Each time you find a new level of awareness and understanding, you are in fact learning the nature of the Way. Consequently, and despite common misperception, the practice of budo is not intended to teach students how to defeat an opponent (a gun would be more efficient), and there are quicker ways to make a good cup of tea than are found in chado. In the Ways, techniques and methods are a vehicle for *seishin tanren*.

Seishin means "spirit" and tanren means "forging." In the Ways, the spirit is forged in a manner not unlike that of a Japanese sword. *Nippon-to*, the sword of the samurai, is world famous for its

Reigi

"Techniques of respect." These are exemplified in bowing and other customs and attitudes in the Ways and Japanese culture aimed at self- and group harmony.

Ryu

Tradition, school, or system of Japanese cultural art with an integrated, comprehensive methodology developed by a founder and perpetuated by his disciples.

incredible strength and amazing sharpness. The sword begins as a lump of iron that is heated, pounded, folded, and beaten into its correct shape. Through this repeated folding and hammering in the red-hot heat of the smith's forge, the Nippon-to emerges. It will eventually be plunged into icy water and tempered, assuming a form that is both beautiful and fearsome.

The sword stood for the soul of the samurai, who sought to shape his very spirit in its image: sharp, resilient, powerful, and pure. Considering the dominant place of the warrior class in Japanese history, it is not surprising that the samurai spirit still permeates Japanese culture, and its arts and Ways, even into the twenty-first century.

The forging of one's spirit is an idea common to all the Do, including the tea ceremony and calligraphy, and certainly the martial arts and Ways, which originally descended from the warrior class. Just as the proper forging of a fine sword demands intense heat and forceful pounding of the smith's hammer, a student of the Way must have his or her spirit purified, strengthened, and sharpened through the practice of the Do, which can seem overly severe until its purpose is understood.

Acquaintances often ask me about the various Do I practice, encouraging me to relate my experiences and explain what practice entails. Depending on the person, and to some degree my mood, I might describe how I regularly practice copying my shodo sensei's calligraphy, maybe even showing a sample of my efforts. They often wonder how many times I have copied a kanji character before achieving the desired result, only to be surprised that my copies don't number in the dozens but more likely in the hundreds. They're even more shocked when I explain that in a single session, I might copy a single stroke of a particular character more than a hundred times—without pause.

Other friends want to know why I go to our dojo on New

Year's Day, especially after a night of partying. I explain I go to practice meditation and breathing exercises with my students of Japanese yoga, which means sitting motionless in seiza in an unheated room for about an hour. These friends, both Japanese and American, who know what it's like to sit in seiza, sometimes grow pale at just the thought of an hour of such "torture."

I sometimes mention *kan geiko*, special training that takes place at the coldest time of the year. The form of kan geiko varies with the art and the teacher, but it is common in budo. In our martial art we go to a nearby beach to train continuously for around three hours. The seaside is cold in the winter, but no warm dress is allowed, just bare feet and a cotton uniform similar to what judo students wear. Once we're "warmed-up," we perform hundreds of throws and falls in the sand.

"Doesn't it hurt?" my friends ask. Yes, but only if you worry about it. "Doesn't sand get in your eyes?" You bet, and into just about every other bodily orifice! But, as severe as it might seem, it's easier than kan geiko undertaken in snow.

Why spend so much time perfecting a single brush stroke? Why not sleep in on New Year's Day? Why on earth would you want to roll around in cold sand or freezing snow just to learn self defense? Such questions inevitably follow.

Starting as a child, however, I was taught to think in terms of seishin tanren. And so, as I explain to my acquaintances, I'm not repeating a single brush movement merely to master a particular stroke. Real mastery of the brush requires self-mastery, and by perfecting my calligraphy, I have a chance to perfect myself—if I approach shodo in the right manner. And this is true of all the Do.

Such self-mastery undeniably demands a tremendous amount of repetition and hard work, but the discipline is something we build up to gradually. At the same time, remember that the mind controls the body, and the body is capable of far more than we give it credit for, especially when it is motivated by a genuinely positive mental state. In the Do, a positive and indomitable attitude is valued and cultivated; reaching it is the martial artist's real motivation for training outdoors in the dead of winter. This is what is meant by seishin tanren.

Finally, it's important to avoid the mistake of excess in the other direction. The concept of seishin tanren has occasionally been used as an excuse in the Japanese arts and Ways for everything from overzealous students, to charging exorbitant fees, to the outright physical abuse of beginners. Returning to the sword analogy, it must be noted that, during the forging process, the sword is certainly exposed to high heat and forcefully beaten, but too much heat or too much force will produce defects; and, during the tempering, immersing the sword for too long or in water that is too cold will likewise introduce defects. Forging a fine sword requires heat and force, but also sensitivity and awareness, and, in the same way, seishin tanren and the practice and study of the Ways require balance and moderation. A student's spirit must be forged but not broken.

Shugyo

If the Ways are vehicles for seishin tanren, it's because the Ways aren't designed solely to provide instruction in a specific activity such as arranging flowers or playing the shakuhachi flute. All of the Ways, given their emphasis on seishin tanren, can be thought of as forms of shugyo.

The term shugyo has quasi-religious overtones and means roughly "austere practices." The sometimes lengthy meditation periods found in Japanese yoga and the martial artist's special winter training are examples of shugyo within the Do forms. Shugyo is an important, inseparable part of the Do, and it also offers something important to contemporary society.

For most of us, our modern, technological way of life has brought us far from the way our ancestors lived. Modern conveniences are a blessing and enable us to live life in comfort and safety. But in premodern times, humanity was necessarily in close connection to nature and inevitably forged toughness and a strong sense of self-reliance. As our lives have grown more comfortable, they have also come to lack a certain mental and physical strength and self-reliance.

The following story illustrates my point. Years ago I heard about a Japanese soldier who had been hiding for years in a remote part of the South Pacific, alone and unaware that World War II was over. Viewing nearby villagers as possible enemies, he always proved elusive when spotted, but he was eventually "captured" and returned to Japan. Once back in Japan, he became an immediate celebrity, and the media interviewed him on several occasions. During one of these interviews, the old man was asked if didn't feel he'd missed out on a lot living in the jungle with only wild animals as his companions. He surprised many by stating that he had gained a great deal from the experience and, contrarily, lost as much by returning to modern Japan.

After years of living in the wild, he discovered that his senses had become heightened, and he had developed a strong connection to his natural surroundings. He could smell the proximity of water and animals even at a distance, he could feel when rain or climatic changes were about to take place, and he could sense the presence of other people well before they were in view.

Back in Japan, however, he was rapidly losing most of these attributes, which in some ways he no longer needed. Moreover, he discovered that ringing phones, construction noise, honking horns, and all the other signs of modern technology frequently

Sabi

An aesthetic characterized by simplicity and austerity, rusticity, serene solitariness, the unevenness brought out in things through time's passage, the worn appearance of objects after long, loving handling but before old age completely destroys them; the feeling evoked by verdigris and patina, autumn, and twilight.

Samisen

*Three-stringed instru-
ment imported to
Japan from China by
way of Okinawa in
the middle of the six-
teenth century. Played
by plucking using a
large "pick."*

were stressful and upsetting to him. His improved medical care and new life in Japan brought him comfort and a welcome return to his homeland, but he had also lost something.

And so have many of us, often without realizing it. Our over-reliance on technological wonders has sometimes destroyed our sense of self-reliance. In the process, I think even our definition of fun has changed from that of our predecessors. In much of American society, for example, hard work is rarely seen as enjoyable. If it's hard, it can't be fun. If it's fun, it isn't work.

Maybe. But what about the great feeling of deep relaxation that sweeps over us like a warm blanket after a long, hard swim? What of the sense of accomplishment found in going beyond our imagined capabilities on a long, tough bike ride? If I were enclosed in a car instead of on my comparatively low-tech bicycle, I'd sweat less, but I'd also fail to see the wild rabbits that lope along beside me and miss the country smells of the rural road I cycle on late at night. Still, one of the most enjoyable things I do is go for a top-down, high-speed drive in an old sports car on a frosty springtime morning, wrapped in a heavy jacket, with the heater blasting and the smell of spring blossoms wafting through the cockpit of my roadster. Wouldn't it be easier to drive with the car top up or not ride a bicycle at all? Sure, but it wouldn't be as much fun.

Similarly, hard physical work outdoors in winter's cold or on a hot summer's day is no longer necessary for many of us, but chopping wood for heat on an icy morning or weeding a vegetable garden under a blazing sun gives us a greater appreciation for warmth and fresh, homegrown food and brings us closer to the natural world around us.

In short, making life too easy tends to take us out of touch with nature itself and our own natures. Of course, we don't want to, and perhaps cannot, eliminate technology in the twenty-first century, but we still need methods to train our minds and bodies, to preserve our link to the natural world. The Japanese arts and Ways can help do this, but only if they are practiced as shugyo.

Most of the Do are decidedly not high-tech. Chado students sit in seiza on relatively hard tatami mats in an old-fashioned tea room that is rarely climate controlled. In the winter, the first warmth they feel during the tea ceremony is when their lips are at long last allowed to touch the frothy green beverage. It might seem harsh, but it is in fact an exquisite experience, one that is markedly different from lounging about in a heated, vibrating massage chair while waiting for the microwave to signal that your instant tea is done.

Turning to budo, in *shochu geiko*, a special training session in summer, martial artists train their minds and bodies to the very limits of their endurance, and beyond, often finding new limits, all during the hottest time of the year. Needless to say, the hall in which this training is done is not air-conditioned.

Japanese gardeners spend many days each week in their niwa, rain or shine, winter and summer, hot and cold. Stooping to prune and cut, they often use methods and tools that are centuries old. Likewise, the late Nakamura Tempu Sensei encouraged his Japanese yoga students to exercise with him wearing only light shorts as a means of "strengthening the skin and training the body to be adaptable." They practiced indoors and out, winter and sum-mer. *Koryu*, or "old style," swordsmanship is also often practiced outdoors in undesirable weather. And shodo students spend hours squatting on the floor in seiza, writing antique Japanese poems with an equally antiquated brush. Calling this low-tech is an understatement.

Such low-tech activities are, however, effective for connect-ing us to the world of wabi-sabi. They bring us back to something very elemental, even spiritual, in character. Within the Do, we connect with truths that are universal but that can easily be lost when life gets too easy or we become too insulated from the natural world. The Japanese Ways give us a means to sustain our innate relationship with nature and rediscover the kind of mental and physical resilience our ancestors possessed. And if we practice Do forms seriously, we don't need to hide out in a South Pacific jungle to achieve this state.

Although the especially intense training of shochu geiko and kan geiko is certainly a form of shugyo, one of my sensei offered a different interpretation related to these rigorous means of seishin tanren: "Shugyo is lifelong daily training in the Way." Compared to meditating under a freezing waterfall or practicing a martial art outdoors in suffocating heat, simply practicing every day over the course of a lifetime doesn't perhaps sound terribly difficult. Those who lightly dismiss daily lifelong practice as not too difficult have likely never studied a Do, and such a view perhaps explains the high drop-out rate among students of the Ways. It's one thing to begin to study a Japanese art, but it's another matter to practice vigorously. It is still another matter to continue to practice. Each day. For the rest of our lives. There are students of kado, chado, and other Ways, who practice extremely hard and rarely miss class—for awhile. The true challenge is to continue past a few months or even a few years of such earnest commitment.

Having discussed this phenomenon over the years with teachers of a wide variety of Do, the conclusion we all seem to have reached is that it is actually more arduous to practice a modest amount daily for a lifetime than it is to engage in severe, special shugyo a few times in your life. Certainly modest daily practice performed throughout life is much more beneficial than a few intense sessions.

Special periods of intensely challenging practice can amount to peak experiences that, though infrequent, can still have a lasting impact on one's life. Nevertheless, particular actions, engaged in as an ordinary part of daily life and repeated over a period of years, penetrate the subconscious, where real learning and understanding take place. After a lifetime of driving a car, for example, how easily could you forget to instinctively depress the clutch when shifting a manual transmission? Such is the value of repeated actions, engaged in as an ordinary part of daily life, over numerous years.

In some Japanese arts, students periodically undergo examinations in order to receive teaching certificates or advance in rank. Although many associate rank with the martial arts, flower arrangement, shodo, and other Do also have ranking schemes. If testing is required for certification, examinations are usually invitational, and the invitation is extended by the sensei. Over time, most students are invited to take such tests—but not all. Some students who are not invited complain that they are certain they could pass the examination if only their sensei would let them take it—and perhaps they could.

But that isn't the point: one teacher I know of tells students that the *real test* takes place each day when they come to train—or when they fail to come to practice. This real test continues during the practice session, when the sensei observes the students' attitudes—toward training, the instructor, their fellow pupils, and ultimately the Way itself. With teachers of this type—and they're common in traditionally practiced Ways—the greatest challenge isn't the examination but receiving the invitation to be examined, and this open door is rarely offered to students who practice irregularly or insincerely, no matter how talented they might be. Along the same lines, engaging in special austerities once a month or once a year is not as difficult, or meaningful, as simply practicing regularly, sincerely, and without giving up.

The discouragement and boredom that sometimes accompany routine practice can be met with the realization that the Ways

Seishin Tanren

Seishin, "spirit," and tanren, "forging," applies the analogy of the shaping and tempering of a Japanese sword to the forging of one's spirit through the practice of a Way.

are most valuable when we're actually engaging in them. The advantages of training in a Do are found in the training process itself, not at some future point. Students of the Way discover the value of their practice in what it does for them as they drill each day and not in relation to some far-off goal. Truly, the Way exists in the present or not at all.

When we let go of training for a future goal, then discouragement isn't a factor. We become discouraged when we think we're not moving quickly enough toward an imagined objective. Doing our best in the moment, however, rarely produces such dissatisfaction. When we realize that we lose many of the benefits of an art if we cease to train in it, we have an added incentive to continue.

Perhaps you've heard someone state that they "know" karate, flower arrangement, or another Japanese art. This reveals a typical Western approach to the Ways that has nothing to do with shugyo. In the Do, having knowledge of a Way is of slight importance. Genuinely practicing a Way and arriving at a deep understanding of what ongoing training does for us over the course of our lives is what is most important. Likewise, to have studied a Way in the past, even rigorously, provides comparatively little benefit in the present. To *actively practice* flower arrangement or tea ceremony on a regular basis brings great spiritual and physical benefits. Our Way has become genuine shugyo, integrated with our daily life, and life itself has become shugyo.

Keiko

Regular *doing* with the full use of our mind and body is the key to successful shugyo, and in the Ways *keiko*, or "practice," is its basis.

In the West, we often speak in terms of having lessons or taking a class in some activity. Such expressions imply something momentary, that the goal is to absorb a set number of lessons and, once accomplished, the class comes to an end. The Do, in sharp contrast to this approach, are not ultimately a series of lessons, and the course has no end, as these disciplines represent a Way of life. Students come together to practice actions they have repeated hundreds of times in the past. New material isn't always introduced, and the teacher is sometimes virtually mute during the training session. Students don't meet with the sensei in order to receive the next lesson in a predetermined series, and the teacher doesn't always introduce the day's "lesson"; it is "found" by pupils in their ongoing repetition of basic patterns of exercise. Learning takes place, but it is frequently on a subconscious, intuitive level, and what is learned is often difficult to verbalize.

As mentioned, sometimes a neophyte will claim to "know" karate or shodo, and of course most use such expressions, not to mean they've fully mastered a given art, but simply that they have knowledge of the general parameters of their Way. In contrast, most Western and Japanese experts will simply say that they "practice" a particular Way, and "practice" is a common translation of keiko.

The term keiko is composed of two parts. The first refers to thinking or the act of reflection, and the second means "antiquity." Since most Ways make use of predetermined patterns of action, forms created at some point in the past and handed down, the ongoing repetition of these patterns involves, in a sense, reflecting on the past. Yet, in the endless repetition of ancient patterns, students discover, through personal experience of these patterns, something new. Take as an example the teacher of a science class, who commonly has students conduct experiments that have been assigned many times in past classes. Although the teacher

Seiza

Literally, "correct sitting." Refers to sitting erect in a kneeling position with the legs tucked beneath the torso and the left big toe resting on top of the right one, with some space between the knees. It is a posture of respect used in the Japanese arts and Ways and for meditation.

Sempai

One's senior in school, place of employment, or in a traditional art, where the term applies to someone with greater experience and expertise. See also kobai; tate shakai.

could simply tell the students what the outcome will be, the students are made to conduct the experiments in order that they will see the results for themselves. Direct, personal, firsthand knowledge arrived at by actually *doing* has much more meaning than a mere intellectual grasp.

In the Ways, students strive for a union of body and mind. Practicing—keiko—established patterns of action, called kata, is not done only in order to master certain techniques but to know and come to embody the principles of the Ways.

Kata

If the Ways can be considered philosophies, then they are "philosophies" with a physical expression, or philosophies discovered through their physical expression. Chado, shodo, kado, and others can be thought of as Ways of art and life whose physical expression is keiko. But what constitutes keiko and why? Let us turn to kata, which are the means through which the Ways are practiced.

Kata means "form," in the sense of a prearranged form or formal pattern. In shodo, students strive to make exact copies of tehon, which are either books of classic calligraphy or samples of their sensei's brush writing. In sumi-e, every novice copies a specific painting and isn't allowed to progress to the next subject of study until the copy is exact. In the tea ceremony, chado disciples must work through a set series of rituals two centuries old, and in the martial Ways, practitioners endlessly repeat established combat sequences.

Yet even in Japan, there are those who claim that, in the martial arts, for example, fixed, predictable kata do not correspond to real-life combat. Similar comments could be made regarding the kata of many Japanese arts, not just budo. And these critics are correct in that the kata of any Do are artificial to the extent they are predetermined. They are incorrect, however, in supposing that practicing kata is inefficient and cannot lead to spontaneous action.

Continuing with our martial arts example, the key is to put aside combat and think in terms of education. Just as struggling with the "story problems" in arithmetic class and repeating over and over scales and "Mary Had a Little Lamb" during piano lessons gave us the rudiments of real-life problem solving and music making, and did so more effectively than if we had been thrown into real-life situations without this preparation, practicing kata in a martial art teaches fundamental principles that can be extrapolated to real life.

Occasionally there is the criticism that some martial arts kata don't feature realistic attacks and combat scenarios. The fallacy in this claim is the presumption that it's possible to predict the nature or form of a future attack. Will it be the bully in the schoolyard using the WWE armlock, or the mugger in the dark alley with the knife? The real deficiency is not in the use of kata in budo but in the practitioner's understanding of the methodology. Budo teachers aren't using kata to teach self-defense, and kata are not a collection of "self-defense tricks" to be memorized. Although many children, and adults too, come to the martial arts in search of secret tricks, and, sadly, many self-proclaimed experts will gladly sell these misguided people such tricks for a high price, there are no secret tricks. Having grown up practicing the Japanese martial arts and once undertaken a search for special techniques that would "really work," I can address this subject with some authority.

Kata are designed to teach principles more than techniques, principles that are universally applicable. These gensoku, fundamental principles, cannot, moreover, be learned intellectually.

Sennin

*Derived from the word
sen, in turn from the
Chinese word hsien,
describes the Japanese
Taoist equivalent to a
yogi. Also variously
translated as "Taoist
immortals," "sages,"
or "mystics." See also
Sennin-do; Sennin
Ryoji.*

They must be learned by doing, which is the role of kata. Repetition of the kata gives us a chance to internalize these principles so that, eventually, we are capable of creating our own variations, or henka, and can thus effectively deal with new situations. In this manner, kan, or "intuitive perception," is cultivated, allowing us to eventually execute and create new or spontaneous techniques that are situation appropriate. This is crucial because we have no idea how we might be attacked; no matter what technique we drill repeatedly, we're still faced with adaptation. Ubiquitous principles can be adapted more broadly and universally than specific memorized techniques.

Another aspect of the rationale behind kata-oriented practice that is crucial relates to an esoteric quality. The founders of many art forms, from tea ceremony to odori, are at times said to have created their art through divine revelation. This kind of enlightenment and the sanctity with which such a tradition is preserved and passed on are by their very nature beyond verbal description. In the Ways, the means for communicating what is beyond words is again the kata, established forms that place the student in situations that require the development of certain attributes. While I can't get you to understand what calmness is simply by telling you what it is, I can place you repeatedly in a situation whose resolution requires the realization of calmness. The same can of course be said for other desired traits—coordination, concentration, and perseverance.

Kata are used and passed on from teacher to student because they have proved to be an effective means of discovering firsthand what is beyond verbal or written description.

Zanshin

As students of the Ways practice kata, they discover that stillness is as important as activity, not doing is equal to doing, and the moment following an action actually determines the success of the action itself, as well as the success of any following actions. This moment is called *zanshin.*

Zan means "lingering," "remaining," and suggests continuation, while shin is simply "mind." Zanshin can be seen in a sumi-e painter's continuing movement of the brush even after it has left the paper. It can be witnessed in a martial artist's freezing of movement after the execution of a final stroke of the sword or jujutsu throw—allowing the action to follow-through and the movement of ki to continue after the technique has been executed. But this pause is pregnant with potential . . . waiting to see if another action will occur or be needed.

Whether in fine art, martial art, or Kabuki drama, zanshin is present. It is a watchful stillness, a stillness that is gestating action. It is not the stillness of the graveyard but of the cat poised motionless before it pounces. There is in zanshin a unity of calm and action manifested in the form of physical presence.

Zanshin can also be observed in a Western context. The follow-through in a bowler's arm movement after the ball has been released and the continued movement of ki down the lane that takes the ball into the pins are examples. The follow-through in a batter's or golfer's swing is another. In all such examples, the instant following the action is as important as the action itself; it is where motion and stillness, doing and not doing merge into oneness.

It is interesting to note that we often fail in an action just at the moment before its completion, when we think we've got it, we have made it. In this instant of broken concentration, our awareness lapses, we fall out of the present moment, and we break our mind-body coordination.

Something I once witnessed at a judo tournament can serve as an example. In judo, a decisive throw garners a full point and thus victory. An imperfect throw, on the other hand, is worth a half point and means that the action continues. At this particular competition, I watched a teenager forcefully throw his opponent, which produced an accompanying roar from the spectators. Perhaps in the din he misheard the referee's assessment of the throw—or maybe he was just positive that he'd won; for whatever reason, he turned, raised his arms overhead, and acknowledged the crowd. Aside from displaying bad manners in traditional budo, the gesture was a very bad idea. The referee had declared the throw a half point, so the action had not yet stopped. The opponent rose from the mat, grabbed the "victor" in a stranglehold, and, falling backward, proceeded to squeeze his neck until he submitted (or fell unconscious; I can't remember which). As the crowd quieted down, I heard an elderly sensei from Japan sitting nearby comment, "Serves him right! Bad manners and no zanshin."

On a related note, my own judo sensei explained that a *judo-ka,* or "judo practitioner," doesn't begin things lightly: if he does start on a certain path, the judoka continues—to death, if need be—despite any obstacles, even if an alternate route must be discovered. And if the judoka dies on the path, his body will always fall in the direction he was going in. Zanshin indeed!

The power of zanshin is eloquently expressed in the arts of Japanese dance and drama. There is a momentary interlude following a gesture or movement during which the full impact, beauty, and drama is able to penetrate the hearts of the audience. The action isn't brought to a standstill, rather its effect is released to linger and reach deep into the witnesses of the performance. Imagine a massive temple bell, struck strongly. An immense, resonant note fades, but something remains, leaving the air charged with an almost electric sensation. . . .

Zanshin is not only the sustained concentration following an action but also an unbroken awareness of the moment and an indomitable spirit; it is the hallmark of all of the Ways, from aikido to shodo to odori.

Okuden

The kata used in the Ways have both visible and hidden elements. These hidden, or "secret," aspects of a kata or ryu are known as *okuden*. *Oku* means "inner," and *den* indicates a "tradition" or "teaching." Okuden have existed in the classical Japanese arts for a variety of historical reasons. Despite what is often assumed by overly romantic writers on this subject, aspects of this phenomenon have not always been especially esoteric or spiritual. In the 1970s, a friend told me of a man he knew in Japan who had just received okuden in the art of bonsai. (Okuden refers in some cases to a rank as well as the transmission of hidden knowledge.) After many years of practice and teaching bonsai, this man was finally initiated into his ryu's innermost principles—for only $10,000!

Why, I asked, would anyone pay such an amount? My friend replied that his acquaintance was quite serious about bonsai, but more, he was a bonsai teacher. And he ran a bonsai nursery. And this was Japan. Which meant, of course, that the acquisition of such knowledge—especially with the high rank attached to it—meant more students, more customers, and more money. It was an investment that would benefit both him and the *iemoto* ("leader") of his bonsai ryu, who received the substantial cash infusion.

153

OKU: *Oku literally means "inner" or "interior," but when it is used in compound words like okuden, it suggests "hidden teachings." Okuden are the vital, yet not always readily apparent, esoteric principles that underlie Japanese art forms. In the various Do, what isn't always obvious is what frequently gives vitality and power to that which can be seen.*

This is an extreme, relatively unusual example. Okuden is often transmitted freely, and teaching titles and ranks in the different ryu aren't invariably expensive. But again, there are exceptions.

Historically, transmitting the kata of a system but not all its inner principles served certain pragmatic purposes. In some cases, a teacher simply wanted to control who knew what. In other instances, the sensei was concerned about who would be ranked at a level where they could teach the more advanced curriculum—quality control at its most basic. In still other examples, an instructor simply might not have wanted too much competition from students who were as well versed as he was. Withholding secret techniques was a means of ensuring supremacy.

Granting that historical precedents and business concerns in Japan may have dictated this approach in the past, and even to some degree today, let's consider the more profound aspects of the okuden concept. In okuden is the implicit recognition that what you see is not all you get. According to in-yo cosmology, if an object has a front, it must have a back; correspondingly, if something can be seen, it must have an aspect that cannot be seen. In our increasingly materialistic high-tech world, with its sound bites, "15 minutes of fame," and a ten-easy-lesson approach to everything from fixing your car to fixing your marriage, it's easy to be persuaded that everything will reveal all aspects of itself instantly and with no personal effort. Because the Ways contain aspects that aren't readily apparent without serious observation, observation conducted by intense personal experience at that, even the simple understanding that okuden exist is a very important insight.

Suppose, for example, I want to explain to my new shodo student how to easily create *kasure*—an attractive effect that allows the white of the paper to show through the ink. I tell him that, as he touches the brush to his paper, he can press downward more strongly than usual, using a slight twist, and then abruptly decrease pressure as he continues the brush stroke to produce a beautiful dry-brush effect in midstroke. This effect causes the hairs to split, so I also explain how to turn the brush slightly on edge to cause the brush to veer off to the left and finish in a fine, smooth, well-defined point. Of course I could explain all this to the student immediately, but it is of little use to tell a new student how to do something that varies from the usual when he has not yet had sufficient experience to grasp what even the "usual" techniques are. Most beginners are struggling with how to hold the brush and make a straight line; asking them to attempt a special effect like kasure only adds unneeded complexity and hinders learning. Obviously a student can be given too much information.

In this sense, a teacher is not simply "withholding certain techniques" but is waiting until a student is advanced enough to be able to appreciate aspects of the art that would have been beyond reach at an earlier stage. Such a hidden point could be small changes in the way rudimentary techniques are performed, changes that might appear minute but that are significant.

Returning to the kasure example, when I do reveal this "secret teaching" at a later time, assuming the student hasn't already figured it out, it may seem to be a revelation and pupils might wonder why it was "held back." However, this misperception is simply the result of an incomplete understanding of okuden. For different cultural and historical reasons, this sort of misperception is not uncommon when Western students study with Japanese sensei,

Sennin Ryoji

Designation used in arcane circles in Japan to indicate healing arts that trace their origins to esoteric Taoism.

and one of my hopes in writing this book is to be able to contribute to the avoidance of such misperceptions.

Instruction in the arts and Ways is often divided into levels, *shoden*, *chuden*, and *okuden*—beginning, intermediate, and advanced. Although some might assume that such levels of instruction relate to degrees of hidden meaning, these stages are as straightforward and logical as grade levels in school. They differ from the comparison, however, in that they are not really hierarchical in scope: each level expresses different parts of a single entity—the Way.

Students at times misunderstand this and decline to enter advanced training, claiming they're not ready, they haven't mastered the basics. Leaving aside the fact that mastery of any Way is an impossibility, in many arts it is only when you learn the advanced methods that you more fully grasp the fundamentals. Advanced training illuminates aspects of the basics that couldn't be seen before—their okuden. Thus the shoden-chuden-okuden process in Do forms describes more a circle than a vertical line, so that an understanding of the fundamentals leads to more advanced methods that in turn refer back to the basics. A pupil's refusal to move on to more advanced levels actually represents a refusal to embrace the totality of practice, and this embrace of its totality is crucial, as the Ways are not only nondualistic but also holistic.

Those are some of the basic points regarding okuden. The concept is not always used by contemporary teachers of the Do, even in Japan. And it is undeniably misused in some cases, although many students report that the acquisition of such new knowledge was meaningful. The important point is that the essence of any Way lies in its fundamentals, and nothing in the universe is truly hidden but is only waiting to be discovered. Serious, steadfast students often uncover okuden for themselves.

On the other side of this, deliberately holding back knowledge can be damaging for a teacher. Hoarding knowledge is ultimately destructive. The universe is infinite; the Way of the universe is infinite, as are the Do, which are particular expressions of the Way of the universe. We learn as long as we believe we have more to learn. Once we begin to store away a limited amount of knowledge, learning comes to a stop. We become like a glass filled to the brim, unable to receive any more. Even if we hang onto what we have, it becomes old, and we wouldn't want to drink a glass of "vintage water." If, on the other hand, we share what we have, we make room for something new.

Let us also consider the student's perspective. Most of us have an attraction toward hidden knowledge, because it seems easier to acquire something we don't have than to change ourselves (as well as our habitual behaviors that hold us back). Gathering knowledge is no different from buying houses, cars, and other items. An envious, greedy person will still be an envious, greedy person even in a million-dollar house or a fancy car. Anyone, within reason, can obtain knowledge. But the realization of wisdom, and the understanding of how to use knowledge, comes only through personal transformation. It has little to do with what we've accumulated, but instead, what we are.

New knowledge, new methods, and the like cannot produce realization. Understanding does not come from outside of us; it cannot be given or bought—not even in the form of okuden.

Omote and Ura

Okuden are present in the Do forms for two reasons: Japanese culture is based on the duality of a "public face" and "hidden face"; and the universe is composed of a similar visible-invisible duality (in-yo). Dualism in the cultural arts of Japan is sometimes

Sensei

Literally one who was "born before," an honorific appellation used after a person's family name to express respectful acknowledgment of his or her rank as teacher in a Japanese cultural art; it is never used when referring to oneself.

Shakuhachi

A bamboo, five-holed, recorder-like flute. The shakuhachi came to Japan from China and has long had certain associations with Buddhism. In some circles, perhaps owing to shakuhachi breath control paralleling meditative breathing exercises, playing the shakuhachi is seen as a form of musical meditation. Students of the flute, as in other traditional Ways, study under a sensei in a particular ryu or school.

referred to as *omote* and *ura*. Omote means "front" or "outside," and ura means "back" or "inside." Omote is what we see; ura, which is just as important or maybe more so, is what is not immediately apparent.

As I've stated, advanced followers of ikebana are not practicing the art simply in order to learn to arrange flowers, devotees of the tea ceremony are not interested only in how to prepare tea, and martial artists are not studying primarily with the aim of self-defense. Subduing an opponent, making tea, and arranging flowers are the omote of budo, chado, and kado. The years of practice and thousands of dollars the study of these arts requires—a commitment of time and money that far exceeds what is necessary to attain a basic mastery of the techniques of these arts—are best understood in relation to the ura of these traditional Ways.

Because I teach a number of Ways, people often ask me to outline the benefits of practice. Long ago, I made a point of emphasizing that the outward forms of these disciplines are only a vehicle (omote) to help students arrive at the genuine goals of deeper concentration, relaxation, willpower, and calmness. These benefits, I explained, are the ura, the real reason for practicing. Over time, however, I realized that these cultivated traits are actually more the by-product of training and not the goal. If we make improved concentration our primary objective, we often miss the essentials of the omote that later lead to discovering this state. Even if we attain improved concentration, we might miss bringing together other vital character traits. The risk in making the by-product the goal is treating the ura as if it were the omote. Nevertheless, it *is* possible to point at the real meaning of practicing a Do, but not in ten minutes over the telephone. When I realized this, I wished for a book I could simply refer people to in order to help them see beyond the omote. So I wrote one.

Although this book isn't the only one that sheds light on

this important aspect of the arts and Ways, there is still a real need for such literature, especially in the West. In Asia, it tends to be understood that the essence of a Do is ultimately beyond description, and the outward forms of practice aren't the only reason for its study. As a result, students are more inclined to look for oku-den, teachings that are not immediately apparent, and to wait for the ura to reveal itself. Because of cultural differences, and because Asian teachers are often disinclined to talk about what can only truly be felt through experience, the Western expression of the different Do sometimes has a distinctly omote flavor. Indeed, in many instances outside of Asia, the more popular Ways have become exceedingly superficial caricatures of their real forms.

However, since omote and ura are simply expressions of the nature of life, we can find omote-ura parallels in Western culture if we look for them. The average person only sees the omote of many things, and without training and intent observation the ura of even something as mundane as a beverage remains incomprehensible or even boring. If you have me sip a fine wine, as someone who doesn't drink, I'll probably just say it tastes like alcohol (omote). Give a wine aficionado the same taste, and he will likely elucidate a world of intoxicating wonders, filled with metaphor and subtle nuances (ura).

Omote and ura, seen and unseen, are telltale signs of the influence of Taoist yin-yang cosmology on a cornucopia of Japanese cultural forms. But more than this, omote and ura reveal the genuine nature of existence. We live in a relative world, made of dualities, and this world stems from a single universe that is absolute. Our relative world/the absolute universe, omote/ura, yin/yang, even heads and tails are part of the same coin that is life. It's not one, not two.

Myo and Yugen

In performing the techniques of a Do, we absorb the Way, using a particular Do as a tool. In the process, we may experience a moment of perfection that is ultimately indescribable. To describe the indescribable, the Japanese arts and Ways use the word *myo*.

Myo indicates something "mysterious," "extraordinary," or "marvelous," but as usual in the Do forms, these words only hint at the actual meaning. Some books on Japanese culture and art mention that myo relates to *ki-in*, that is a "spiritual rhythm," or more literally, "the rhythm of ki." In short, ki-in describes a sensitivity to and harmony with ki on all levels. When an ikebana artist senses and unites with the rhythm of the ki of nature, she displays the very essence of the universe in art. If she perceives the rhythm and alternation of the ki of plants and blossoms—their growth, decline, and death, how they change in form and feeling with the seasons—then she can successfully arrange flowers. In her practice of kado, she liberates the spirit of all flowers, indeed the spirit of nature itself. In Japanese ink painting or calligraphy, when an artist can sustain the even, rhythmic flow of ki and attention in his craft, then a unity of mind and body results and so does art. In such a case, shodo becomes more than skillfully rendered lines on paper: the artwork displays a life-affirming rhythm and movement that reverberate ki-in and myo even centuries after its creation.

Ki-in, then, relates to the rhythm of ki on personal and impersonal levels. Every activity has its unique rhythm; even actions that we don't think of as rhythmic (such as the act of writing) have a rhythm to them that can't always be seen but that can be sensed. Part of this rhythm that relates to myo is what budo authority Karl Scott Sensei has termed "right place, right time, right frame of mind." When we sense and sustain the right and natural rhythm for a given activity, at the right place and at the right time, myo is the result.

Relating to and further elucidating myo is the word *yugen*. Yugen suggests something "cloudy," "unfathomable." Yet this cloudiness is not out and out darkness but instead a state beyond the limits of intellectualization. But not beyond the capacity of human experience.

Although difficult to describe, yugen can be felt, just as we can sense the blueness of the sky even when clouds obscure it. Likewise, we shouldn't imagine that the unfathomable essence of myo and yugen makes their experience less meaningful. The ultimate nature of life and of the infinite universe itself is beyond the intellect, but this doesn't make our feeling of wonder any less meaningful.

It is in a state of mind and body unification, a state of self-harmony and universal harmony, that all Do function at a high level. When this condition expresses itself in art, it produces actions and works that resonate a palpable movement or vibration: ki-in. The effect and sensation produced transcend words and are, in this sense, mysterious (myo). This state gives us a momentary peek into the enigmatic world of yugen, which is a world that encompasses the totality of existence, life on every level, mundane and lofty. For serious students of the Way, this quality is sometimes experienced in actions that might seem commonplace. This is to be expected, in that the Ways concern themselves with living our daily lives wholeheartedly more than with otherworldly concerns.

Myo elevates simple acts of the tea ceremony, shodo, or budo into bona fide art. It imparts a palpable aura to these arts when they are expertly performed that is noticeable but still indescribable. In the case of myo, it isn't what you do as much as how you do it that's vital, or maybe what we do and how we do it are equally important. But not everyone sees this, just as not everyone notices an indescribable cloud formation that's disappearing as rapidly as it formed.

A few illustrations will help clarify the nature of myo and yugen. In the 1980s, I participated in my first Kokusai Shodo-ten, an international exhibition of calligraphic art sponsored by the Kokusai Shodo Bunka Koryu Kyokai. My teacher is the vice-president of the group, and he and I were to receive awards, so we met up at the exhibition in Urayasu, near Tokyo.

Sensei suggested we have lunch with Ueno Chikushu Sensei, the president of the Kokusai Shodo Bunka Koryu Kyokai. Ueno Sensei was diabetic, very elderly, and rather frail. During lunch, I suddenly realized that Ueno Sensei had been holding a heavy plate for me to take. Despite toothpick-thin arms, his hand never wobbled. As we ate, I watched him use his chopsticks and hold his cup of tea. I never detected the slightest shaking in his hands. When I mentioned this observation to my teacher, Sensei shrugged and said, "Lots of shodo practice." In this simple comment we find the birthplace of myo.

Another example concerns my struggle to get a more powerful feeling in my calligraphy without sacrificing equanimity in the characters. During one particular class, I saw Kobara Ranseki Sensei, my teacher, execute, without the slightest hesitation, a single, decisive brush stroke that powerfully evoked myo in shodo. To a casual onlooker it might have seemed to be nothing more than a quick flick of the brush; but to me, someone who had many times tried to produce this particular and powerful brush stroke, it was much more. As Sensei conducted the lesson that day, he periodically made the stroke again under different circumstances. It was always the same: resolutely powerful but completely composed, and invariably in the identical, correct spot—each and every time. More remarkable still was that he occasionally executed this action while talking to students, sometimes without even looking at the paper. I never asked Kobara Sensei about this striking ability because I knew what his response would be: "Lots of shodo practice." Ever hear the saying that the secret's in the little things? So is myo.

Mu

Just as the experience of myo eludes ready description, the essence of the absolute universe defies naming. In the Do, which are specific expressions of the Way of the universe, the word *mu* is used to suggest the nature of the universe. Relating but not limited to Buddhism, mu means "the void," "nothingness," with both cosmic and mundane nuances.

Mu is the unknown, but not an unknown outside human experience; as ever-changing and ultimately unknowable aspects of it, we ourselves belong to the unknown. And mu is a void, but the void isn't empty. Something that encompasses everything thus engulfs nothing, not one thing but all things. If I exist as part of everything, then the individual I dissolves into the totality of all things. "I don't exist" means everything exists. "Everything exists" means I exist. I am nothing; I am everything. I am the universe; the universe is myself.

Kenneth Yasuda, in *The Japanese Haiku*, explains:

> When one happens to see a beautiful sunset or a lovely flower, for instance, one is often so delighted that one merely stands still. This state of mind might be called

Shinto

"The Way of the gods." Shinto is an indigenous Japanese form of worship centered on a reverence for all aspects of nature, including one's ancestors. Central is the idea that all creations have their own kami, or "divine beings."

Many kami are thought to have protective capacities. From Shinto, the Ways drew their emphasis on "purity" and purification well as a naturalistic emphasis in the form of practice, the style of the practice itself, and the aesthetics of the Do. Sabi ("rusticity") and wabi ("simplicity"), while inspired by Zen, have Shinto overtones. See also sabi; wabi.

"ah-ness," for the beholder can only give one breath-long exclamation of delight: "Ah!" The object has seized him and he is aware only of the shapes, the colors, and the shadows. . . . there is here explicitly no time or place for reflections for judgements or for the observer's feelings.[13]

Nakamura Tempu Sensei conceived the same idea while living in the shadows of the Himalayas, and in his Shin-shin-toitsu-do system of Japanese yoga, he called it muga ichi-nen: "no self, one thought." Referring to Yasuda's example, the sunset is one thought, one experience, in which the experiencer and the experience merge. At that instant of union, there is no self-consciousness, which would pull the experiencer away from the experience itself; the moment of "ah-ness" can be fully experienced only when we cease to exist apart from the experience itself. This is muga.

In the Ways, the qualities that are cultivated, such as the faculty of concentration, in order to arrive at muga ichi-nen are as meaningful as the aim itself. In order to focus ki in an activity and reach muga ichi-nen, we must discover how to keep our mind free of distracting thoughts and outside stimuli; if the mind is arrested by a sound or thought, it can no longer be centered on making tea, arranging flowers, or playing the shakuhachi. Even using the mind to free itself is a distraction.

Imagine sitting in a crowded, noisy restaurant and suddenly noticing a fire break out in a building across from the restautant. While you are concentrating on the fire you do not look at the people around you or listen to the sounds in the restaurant; they are a part of your awareness, but your focus is entirely on the fire. In the state of muga ichi-nen, exterior stimuli and internal thoughts are the passing people, and fire is the artistic activity— the one thought. We "watch" the moment, and "do nothing." In meditation, whatever thoughts or internal conflicts come up—*do nothing.* Don't try to force them to stop or change. And don't do nothing to still the mind, silence fears, or resolve conflicts—all of this is *doing something.* It leads to more struggling and hampers us from seeing the actual nature of thought and internal conflict. Genuine attention has no motive.

MU: *"The Void." Painted in the cursive* sosho *style of the renowned calligrapher Chiei.*

Concentrated observation or listening doesn't involve effort. Effort distracts us from what is taking place in the instant. The effortless concentration that occurs when one is "lost" in rapt attention to a moving piece of music or compelling story, or the spectacle of a raging fire, is by its nature unforced.

This idea of effortlessness correlates to mui, which is a term believed to be borrowed from Taoism. Yoel Hoffman, in *Japanese Death Poems,* defines it as follows:

> Taoists define correct behavior as "non-action" (Ch., wu wei; Jp., mui), which does not mean "sit still and do nothing." Rather, it refers to action in which natural processes are not interfered with—actions as natural as the growth of sunflowers.[14]

The author rightly explains that sunflowers grow tall according to their nature; we don't need to pull up on them everyday to make this happen. In the case of seated meditation, mui does indeed mean to "sit still and do nothing," but the intent here is to illustrate that "doing nothing" doesn't necessarily mean, "don't do anything." It is in the nature of sunflowers to grow tall and no effort is required to make them do so.

Shizenteki

Quality of "natural-ness" and reverence for nature central to Japanese art and traditional culture.

The concept of mu is not exclusively Taoist, and parallels can also be found in Buddhism. There is a well-known sutra that mentions form becoming empty and emptiness (*ku*) assuming form. This emptiness is alternately characterized as ku or mu, which have roughly the same meaning.

The notion of emptiness and form in this sutra has found expression in the Ways. Ikebana, for example, is not only the arrangement of flowers and branches but also the arrangement of empty space. When I studied bonsai, I was told to prune and create enough space between the tree's branches so that a miniature bird could fly through the bonsai. This attention to space, what Western art refers to as negative space, is important in all the arts and Ways, and in Japanese culture generally. Again, the experience of the meaningfulness of space is universally available.

We're often made aware of something by its very absence. For example, I live at the entrance to a valley in a rural area. At the right season, the sound of crickets fills the night air. Because the sound is so ubiquitous, it's often unnoticed. Yet, when I ride my bicycle in the valley late at night, my presence causes the trill of the crickets to suddenly cease. And it is in this emptiness of sound that I occasionally first hear the crickets' song.

In Japanese art, a harmonious balance between form and emptiness, in-yo, yin-yang, is essential. Reality, as the Greek philosopher Heraclitus observed, ultimately contains no opposites, and in the Do we see a seamless joining of emptiness and substance that reflects life itself. A novice in a Japanese art has a free, enthusiastic beginner's mind but little skill in technique. Later, with the accumulation of knowledge and skill, self-consciousness and a lack of spontaneity can arise. But if the student continues, the underlying principles of the art are internalized and the practitioner returns to the beginner's mind. The expert, or meijin, began in an unformed state, acquired form, then returned to a condition of formlessness. No form to form to no form, as expressed in the Hannya Shingyo Sutra: *Shiki soku ze ku, ku soku ze shiki,* "From form to emptiness, and from emptiness to form."

Sen no Rikyu, founder of the tea ceremony as practiced today and greatly influenced by Zen, expresses the concept as follows:*

Keiko to wa
Ichi yori narai
Ju o shiri
Ju yori kaeru
Moto no sono ichi.

In your practice
Start by learning one
And continue until you understand ten.
From ten you must return
To the original one.

In the sixth century, the Indian sage Nagarjuna wrote of the Madhyamika sect of Buddhism and pointed to mu. Like most early Buddhists, he espoused the interdependence of all creations. If everything exists in relationship to everything else, for Nagarjuna, no one thing existed solely in and of itself. In other words, you, every other entity, and me are defined as distinct by comparison with that which we are not. And without the other, no such distinction can be made. We are everything. We are nothing.

Mu.

---

* Rikyu imbued cha no yu with a spiritual sensibility that had sometimes been previously lacking. Zen in particular is associated with use of the word "mu." *Mushin* ("no mind") and *munen* ("no thoughts") are terms common to Zen and the Ways.

MUSHIN KORE DOJO: "The empty mind is the true dojo." Mushin, meaning literally "no mind" or "empty mind," is easily misunderstood. It describes a state in which the mind is like a mirror: it reflects everything as it really is, but without clinging to any particular reflection. The mirror can do this due to its emptiness, yet the mirror isn't exactly empty—it always reflects something. A mind that is empty of conditioning, delusion, and attachments is free to reflect the actual Way of the universe. In doing so, the mind discovers the true dojo, or "place of the Way."

Chapter 4

FOLLOWING
THE WAY

In writing this book, I've considered three types of readers: those who are studying a Do and understand it as a Way, those studying a Do but who don't understand it as a Way, and those who haven't studied a Do and aren't familiar with the practice of a Japanese art as a Way of life. In two of three cases, therefore, I'm writing for readers who haven't experienced the practice of a Japanese art as a spiritual path, and this chapter is aimed especially at this larger group of readers.

It might surprise you that someone could practice, and in too many cases actually teach, a Do form without realizing what it means to genuinely engage in it as a Way. Human beings frequently do things in a mechanical manner, unaware of what is taking place at the moment. Along with this tendency is the habit of making assumptions. It's common to assume that because we're practicing an art that ends in "Do" and our teacher is tossing off Asian-sounding platitudes that we are seriously investigating the nature of the Way. Assumptions, however, are based on the past, and reality is now and rarely matches our assumptions about it. We study the Ways to wake up to reality.

Because seeing reality for ourselves is potentially a scary business, many of us rely on the words and opinions of others to describe the nature of the universe and ourselves. The inclination to rely on what others say exists perhaps because we fear seeing things we would rather not see, which in turn could cause major upheavals in our lives. Real change involves stepping into the unknown, and the unknown can fill us with fear because we cling to a mistaken belief in an unchanging world.

Why we depend on what others say and fear seeing the true nature of the universe are important questions, but don't take my word for it. Ask the questions of yourself, find out if they are valid, and without assuming, look into what is taking place around you at this instant.

What is exists only in the moment. That is indisputable, as both the past and the future have no genuine existence except in our imaginations. Yet our minds are more often in the past or future than in the present. We worry about what we did or about what might happen down the road. We worry without realizing that worry itself only takes place in the past or future: the moment contains no time or space for worrying—only action. When you worry about something, is your mind in the present or is it in the past or future?

The Ways don't involve philosophical speculation but actually doing something, whether painting, serving tea, or engaging an opponent. And doing exists in the moment, as does the body, thus offering us a chance to explore unification of mind and body in the instant. It would be difficult to image a more valuable exploration.

It is obvious from the preceding that we cannot learn the Ways or discover the Way by reading about them. Nevertheless, books can point at universal truths. They can also inspire readers to take up the practice of a Do form. Perhaps most important, they can ask questions that cause us, writer and reader alike, to drop preconceived ideas about living, giving us, in that way, the opportunity to experience the beauty of existence as it really is.

So now you might be thinking about practicing a Do that has always fascinated you. You might go to the Yellow Pages or World Wide Web to find a suitable teacher and school. This might or might not be a useful method. Many genuine teachers are not in the Yellow Pages or on the Web. And in the Japanese Do, there are no teachers, only sensei. And sensei do not have schools or studios or gyms. And they don't have students, they have *deshi*, and deshi don't take classes. Confused? Let me explain.

Taking Classes versus Joining a Dojo

We live in a consumer-oriented world. It seems almost everything—and sometimes everyone—is for sale. When it comes to learning something, we expect to find a school, pay for classes, and get what we paid for. This works if you're taking a course in math. You pay for the finite series of classes, buy the textbook, listen to the teacher explain the material in the text, take the test, and you complete the course. You got what you paid for. But a dojo isn't a math class. The sensei cannot be bought. The course never ends. And the Way is not for sale.

I once had someone visit our dojo to observe group practice in one of the Do we study. He wanted to take only private lessons from me; however, the art he was interested in requires interaction with a variety of people if a person is to learn it well. I explained this and offered to teach him privately as long as he participated in some group instruction. He left promising to think about it.

I got a call from him a week later reiterating his desire for only private lessons. I also repeated my explanation, adding that, although I'd certainly bring in more money by teaching him privately, I'd also be doing both of us a disservice. He offered even more money. I declined. At this juncture he grew incensed, unable to understand that money wasn't the issue. It might have been the first time he had been faced with something he couldn't buy—for any price. Isn't the customer always right? Perhaps. But a dojo isn't a convenience store. The Way is not for sale.

Similarly, I've had people visit who had made long-term com-

Shochu Geiko

Special summer training during which martial artists (and practitioners of some other Do forms) train their minds and bodies to the limits of their endurance and beyond in order to find new limits. See also shugyo.

Shodo

The Way of calligraphy, an ancient art valued as a visual art form but also as a form of "moving meditation" and as a means to enhance concentration, willpower, and poise. The pictographic nature of Chinese characters lends shodo a quality in common with abstract art.

mitments to another sensei and another version of one of the Ways I practice. I usually encourage such people to honor their original commitment and continue with what they've started. For most, the additional time commitment alone would make sincere study at our dojo difficult. On more than one occasion, the person has been dumbstruck that I was sending them away: "But you're offering classes, and I'm prepared to sign up and give you my money." The Way is not for sale.

A sensei isn't selling the Way, and so he or she doesn't have customers. A dojo is not an enterprise designed to make money. It certainly can be run in a businesslike, professional manner, and in some cases it may be prosperous. The fundamental intent of a dojo, however, differs from a business or school.

"Dojo" is a term originally used for an area in a Buddhist temple employed for meditation. Do means "the Way," and *jo* means "place." The original Sanskrit term is *bodhimandala*, meaning "the place of enlightenment." The word for "school" in Japanese is *gakko*. Although many people assume that a dojo refers to a martial arts training hall, in fact dojo are not limited to budo. Not too far from our dojo, for example, is the world-renowned San Francisco Taiko Dojo. They practice the Way of the *taiko* drum, which is hardly a martial art.

A dojo, then, is an environment where firsthand experience and experimentation lead to deep understanding. The memorized data or theoretical understanding of a subject associated with a classroom setting are actually of a secondhand nature. What is secondhand is in effect borrowed; it isn't genuinely part of us since we haven't experienced it for ourselves. In the Ways, understanding comes from what we sense for ourselves by means of direct mind and body experience, and the place for this experience and understanding is the dojo.

Teachers versus Sensei

Sensei is a title of respect that is widely used in Japan. It means "teacher," but it connotes ideas not necessarily suggested by the Western notion of teacher. Because of a lack of knowledge of Japanese culture in general and the Ways in particular, misconceptions regarding the sensei as a concept and as an actual individual have crept into American and European understanding of the Do.

On the one hand, the sensei of the classical Ways are not equivalent to, for example, a high school teacher; the methods and place of instruction, for one thing, differ significantly. On the other hand, "sensei" shouldn't be taken to mean infallible master, cult leader, or Grand Pooh-Bah. Sensei is also not a designation reserved for teachers of ikebana, karate, or a particular Japanese art. In fact, doctors, lawyers, and certain other professionals receive the same designation. It's possible to suggest that a doctor, for example, is teaching the Way of medicine, but this understanding of teaching differs from that in the West.

Likewise, the assumption occasionally encountered in the United States that you can only have one sensei is patently false. Considering the broad usage of the term in Japan, this is obviously a Western myth. It is true that sensei will caution that trying to seriously follow several Do forms is frequently a mistake. Owing to the time needed to seriously study such arts, even practicing more than one is likely to be too much for busy people. Little is gained from studying too many Do; they are all aspects of a single universal Way. The point of practicing one Do is to follow *the* Do, not to acquire a diversity of technical knowledge or intellectual entertainment. Teachers in Japan also warn that having more than one sensei *for a specific art* can be a problem. Attempting, for example, to practice two systems of flower arrangement simultaneously can lead to confusion, not to mention serious conflicts of interest.

Shogi

Like the game go, sho-gi was brought to Japan from China centuries ago. Two participants play on a board made up of eighty-one squares. Somewhat similar to chess, the objective is to immobilize the other person's "king" and capture him. Each contestant has twenty pieces, which have eight distinct stand-ings. Shogi offers a series of ranks (dan), and like go, is thought to cultivate concentra-tion and mental power.

In this context, it is true that you can only have one sensei, but there are many sensei. So if you were to visit another teacher of flower arrangement, regardless of the system, and you failed to call him or her Sensei, you would be considered rude by that teacher and also by your own sensei.

Despite this, I've heard people in the United States refuse to call anyone Sensei other than their own teacher. Others some-times even refuse to call their own teacher Sensei "until I'm sure I respect you enough to offer you that title." Beyond seeming bizarre to anyone who has studied a Way in Japan, these attitudes point to a misconception. Such people take their sensei and the title itself far too seriously. They are looking for a perfected being who will confer on them the Truth. This is fantasy. Skilled sensei of the Do point the way by passing on knowledge and creating an environment where students are able to arrive at a direct under-standing through their own efforts and motivation.

At the other extreme, there are people who refuse to address their teacher as Sensei because "It's no big deal," "This is Ameri-ca," or because they simply can't be bothered. This attitude negates the distinctive relationship that exists in the Do between sensei and student. Although you might have little or no contact with your sensei outside the dojo, your relationship with him or her is not an impersonal one, "just business." Because of the spir-itual and life-altering nature of the Ways, sincere study under an equally serious sensei produces a unique and close alliance. I've rarely socialized with some of my sensei, but, owing to the pene-trating and long-term characteristics of our relationship, my sen-sei frequently know me better than some of my close friends do. My teachers might not know my favorite food, owing to a certain distance often needed in such relationships, but they have none-theless plumbed the depths of my personality in a manner seldom encountered. (As sensei to my students, I have seen the counterpart to this.) If, therefore, I were to address my teachers by their first name, it would serve only to negate the special nature of the connection in the Ways between sensei and pupil. As significant, it would also reveal the superficiality of my intent. (This relationship isn't always paralleled in Japan between, for instance, a lawyer and his client, although the lawyer would be addressed as Sensei.)

As in life in general, a correct balance is needed in studying the Ways. Our sensei isn't a god, but we also don't have the kind of relationship with her or him that we have with our buddies or our sixth-grade teacher. This is because we are not classroom students; we are not taking classes or attending school, and we are not trying to simply acquire technical knowledge. We are interested in seeing and embracing the Way.

Students versus Deshi

A student who pays for a college or evening class is, in a sense, a consumer. In Japanese, *seito* is the term used to refer to this kind of student. A "student" of a Do form in Japanese is called a deshi, a word that is perhaps closer in meaning to the old Western concept of an apprentice. Since the Way is not for sale, and a dojo isn't merely a business, deshi don't actually take classes or pay tuition. (This is not to say that dojo don't charge a fee, they usually do, but the fee is more a donation to help sustain the operation of the dojo and support its sensei.)

Students *attend* a class and expect to be taught. Deshi *join* a dojo to discover and embrace a Way. Joining a dojo is closer to being adopted into a family than attending a class. Students seek information. Deshi make a commitment to undergoing transformation and gaining understanding. Students memorize facts; deshi

Shoshin

"Beginner's mind." Believed to be derived from Zen, it describes a state of mind that always remains fresh, never bogged down by its own past. With shoshin, the student is able to look at each practice session in an art as if it were being experienced for the very first time.

learn through practice. To learn is to grow, and to grow is to change. Are we seeking actual growth, and thus change, or are we more interested in intellectual stimulation and/or the redecoration of what we already are? For the deshi, this is a key consideration.

When I first started to teach the Shin-shin-toitsu-do style of Japanese yoga, I noticed an interesting and ongoing occurrence. The principles of mind and body unification underlying this Way are universal, relating to a variety of people and subjects. Consequently, certain students would invariably enthuse that I was saying things they had always believed or introducing things they had always thought possible. Although such enthusiasm might seem harmless, it isn't always a good thing.

Some of these ardent participants dropped out as quickly as they had started, more quickly than many other people. I began to ask myself what might occur if I said something they haven't heard before, if they were challenged in what they believe or were required to consider real change. I discovered that such students are ardent if they feel I am confirming their beliefs or expectations and much less so when I surprise or challenge them. This phenomenon is not limited to my dojo.

Are we in fact looking for authentic growth, which is change, or just seeking confirmation of what we have already experienced? Do we seek escape from the prison cell of stagnation or only a redecoration of that cell?

If we have reoccurring problems, these problems repeat because we are carrying previous conditioning, and *what we were*, from the past into the present. This affects *what we are*. To break this cycle requires a break with the past, a break with the known and a leap into the unknown. The dojo, ourselves, the sensei all exist in the present. Clinging to the past in the form of beliefs, biases—conditioning of any kind—transforms the present into another version of our past. Certainly exposure to new, radically different ideas can forever change *what we think*, but the Ways continuously change *what we are*.

The Do or Tao is the Way of the universe, a Way that always exists in the present, changing and not changing, from moment to moment. Embracing the Way, then, invites freedom in continuous change and never-ending growth. Can such a Way be discovered by a mind that is conditioned by its own past and thus locked in a loop, a loop that it can modify but not escape? Freedom lies in adaptability to circumstances, and adaptability exists in a mind that embraces the ever-changing moment, a moment that has never existed before and that is by its very nature unknown, and thus filled with infinite possibilities.

Accumulated knowledge is not understanding. Humankind has accumulated knowledge from the past for generations. Although useful, it has not deeply transformed humanity: war, racism, and poverty still exist. Understanding is realized from moment to moment. The moment is eternal, existing beyond time. The Way is likewise eternal and transcendent.

Reigi

What I have described in the preceding does not exist in the West or in Japan without exception. Some sensei see themselves as teachers with students and schools, and not all sensei describe their place of practice as a dojo and their students as deshi. Nonetheless, what I have described reveals the traditional approach to practice of the Ways, and an awareness of this approach will be of value to students who find themselves in traditional or more westernized settings. Certainly an idea of what can be expected in the more traditional dojo will lessen the likelihood of "culture shock."

Shugyo

Containing quasi-religious overtones, shugyo means roughly "austere practices." The Ways, with their emphasis on "spiritual forging," are themselves shugyo. The occasionally long meditation periods in Japanese yoga and the martial artist's special winter training are examples of shugyo in the Do. See also kan geiko; shochu geiko.

Soji

Ritualistic cleaning of the training hall. From Shinto, the Ways drew their traditional emphasis on purity and various purification practices (misogi). Cleanliness and purity are closely connected. Whether you visit a martial arts dojo or a school of calligraphy in Japan, it's common to see students engaging in soji. Soji relates as much to the purification of the individual as it does to the tidiness of a practice area. See also misogi.

And culture shock is not too strong a term to use. Since many sensei are Japanese or are Westerners who have trained in Japan and know they are dealing with important Japanese cultural properties, you may wonder if, when you step into their dojo, you've suddenly entered a foreign environment. Even if your new sensei goes to lengths to make you feel at home or to explain her teachings in a manner understandable to Westerners and novices, don't assume that she is the same as a schoolteacher. Most sincere sensei are nice people, and Japanese culture is gracious toward new acquaintances. These impressions can lull you into thinking that your dojo isn't that different from your tennis club. If you've found an authentic dojo and a genuine sensei, this assumption couldn't be more wrong.

Like any culture, the dojo has its own means of functioning that may not be familiar or compatible to you. Indeed, because the culture of the dojo is not necessarily the same as that of modern Japan, even Japanese can suffer from a sort of culture shock. Yet among the valuable aspects of training in a Do is cultural exchange itself, and it's only clinging to what we're comfortable with that can make this experience a negative one. What's more, the different culture you're moving into isn't different simply because of its Japanese overtones. The greatest, most important, and yet most subtle difference lies in the culture of the Way itself, which doesn't always conform to current social norms.

In Japan generally and in the dojo in particular, the means of harmoniously interacting with a sensei and other deshi are called reigi, "techniques of respect." Reigi is often translated as "etiquette," but I feel this trivializes the concept.

Its most common expression is the traditional Japanese bow. Bowing and other behavioral aspects of reigi will be explored momentarily. For now, however, I'd like to stress that this explanation of reigi is my own; repeating what others have written is of little interest to me or the reader. My description of reigi is based on spiritual concepts I have defined in this book, and in that sense transcends culture. Of course other interpretations, from a historical or social point of view, are viable, but my orientation is primarily spiritual.

The Spirit of Reigi

All creatures originate from the universe and, in a spiritual sense, are manifestations of its creative impulse. We come from the same origins and return to the same state at death. In this view, we are linked with one another and all things in the universe. When life is viewed holistically, all people, plants, and animals deserve respect. To respect others means respecting ourselves, for we exist by the grace of nature and its vital ki. Ideally, reigi in the Ways, if not always in Japanese society, embodies techniques to demonstrate and explore respect—*rei*—for all things. Serious exploration of this respect could perhaps lead to a discovery of our oneness with the universe. (Although the phrase "oneness with the universe" has been so frequently used as to become a cliché, such an important human exploration is anything but cliché.)

It isn't uncommon in Japan to hear experts in the Ways state that "Such-and-such a Do begins and ends with *rei*." In the case of the tea ceremony, for example, one of the most influential Ways, respect for fellow participants and nature is considered paramount. Confirming this are the four essentials of chado: harmony, respect, purity, and tranquillity, which are in fact valued in most Ways.

Western students of the Do, however, sometimes think that reigi simply refers to bowing. Of course, rei does mean "bow," but it also means "respect," thus indicating a correlation between the two. More important, rei meaning both bow and respect demonstrates a historical inclination to not divide the mind and body, thoughts and actions, in the Ways (if not in Japan in general). Bowing is, however, one of many physical expressions of reigi that is not more important than the attitude underlying it. In order to understand the essence of the Do and reigi, it is important to look deeply into their ultimate implications as well as their current expressions.

It might come as a surprise to know that such serious consideration of reigi and other aspects of the Ways does not invariably occur in Japan. For many Japanese a bow is a bow, and reigi amounts to a social custom. This sort of taking things for granted is perhaps not really unexpected; it's not unlike the way we in the West take the handshake and its implications for granted. How often is this gesture performed sincerely, mindfully? Japanese culture is no different in this sense. For this reason, a number of experienced Western (and in some cases Japanese) teachers of the Do believe that the Ways may make a leap in growth now that they have been transplanted in the West. Why? Because they're foreign to us, we don't take them for granted. This refers, of course, to earnest Western students of the Do who have tried to see beyond the external form of the Ways, their omote.

The martial Way of aikido is an example of this phenomenon. Several prominent aikido teachers in Japan and the United States have commented on how Westerners are more inclined to look into the spiritual side of what is widely touted as the most spiritual form of budo. In Japan, they complain, pupils often view it as a hobby, health-maintenance program, or social activity. And these days, more people are practicing aikido outside of Japan than in it. Likewise, tea ceremony practitioners, in both East and West, grumble about how chado has become nothing more than a "finishing school" for young Japanese women who want to be seen as cultured in order to improve their marriage prospects.

Before we pull a muscle from excessive back patting, it must be pointed out that, although this phenomenon certainly exists, many Westerners lack an understanding of how aikido, chado, and other Do function as Ways. Even fewer realize the manner in which reigi works as more than etiquette. Further, it's admittedly simplistic to think that because Japanese students don't sit around philosophizing about their art, as Westerners are sometimes overly inclined to do, it means they aren't serious about its spiritual side. Still, owing to our lack of familiarity with such Ways and customs, the potential for a renewed, reinvigorated examination of the Ways (and reigi) is possible. Whether this potential is realized is up to people like you and me.

Although it is certainly true that ultimately the deepest roots of the Do lie in the human heart, where there are no nationalities or borders, in order to understand the meaning of reigi and the Do more generally it is worthwhile exploring their Japanese cultural context.

The Tradition of Sempai-Kohai

To understand Japanese culture, we must grasp *tate shakai*, or "vertical (or class) society." Japanese society is based on a system Westerners might compare to the relationship between a parent and child. It defines relationships between employer and employee, teacher and student—indeed, virtually all relationships in Japan. Ideally, it's not so much a system of strict hierarchical relationships as one of mutual service, duty, patronage, and respect, alternating from one level to the other and back again.

According to this model, just as a child follows and respects a parent, Japanese adopt this same attitude toward, for example, a teacher, religious leader, and, to some degree, even an employer. A

Suiseki

An art symbolizing natural phenomena, from countryside to the universe, using a stone a few inches to a foot and a half in dimension. Suiseki begins with the discovery and acquisition of stones in nature and consummates in a sensation of beauty as well as a spiritual connection between the collector and the stone. An ideal suiseki pleases the eye, yet kindles wonder as it duplicates a mountain in small scale. It can also function as a spiritual and reflective form, a stone allegory that helps us identify with and comprehend things of value.

Tachi-rei

*A "standing bow."
Bowing is a common
expression of respect in
the Ways and can be
a means of practicing
the coordination of
mind and body. The
manner in which bow-
ing is performed will
vary in depth and
duration—depending
on the social situation.
Deeper angles, held
longer, are considered
more formal and sig-
nificant. Za-rei, the
"seated bow" is also
more formal.*

primary example of this "parent-child" attitude is the tradition of
sempai-kohai, or "senior-junior," which is found in traditional
dojo and Japanese society generally. Sempai are individuals who
have studied, trained, or worked for a longer period and have more
experience than their juniors. A person who is employed ahead of
you in a company, for instance, is your sempai and is treated
accordingly. Many relationships within the dojo and in life can be
described in terms of this relationship.

Westerners might have difficulty understanding this concept
since relationships in Western societies are less hierarchical. But,
rather than comparing one model to the other, it might be most
useful to accept that the nature of relationships in Japanese and
Western societies differs, and to recognize that, in this relative
world, it is sometimes necessary to accept relationships according
to such categories as senior and junior. In the absolute universe,
every duality ultimately reduces to one. But we live in a relative
world, where life is split into opposites. In recognizing our unity
with the universe, we realize that dualities like sempai-kohai are
actually complementary and form one harmonious whole.

In life and in the dojo, sempai should care for and respect
their kohai while helping them to develop. Conversely, kohai
should show support for their sempai while attending to their
needs. This mutual relationship is upheld by reigi and embodies
forms of etiquette such as bowing to seniors, cleaning, and maintaining the dojo, as well as possessing an attitude that accords with
reigi. Although deference and respect are shown to everyone in
the dojo and outside, students who are most senior and closest to
the sensei often receive more elaborate displays of respect, just as
planets closest to the sun receive the most sunlight.

This may be easier for Westerners to comprehend if they
realize that kohai show respect to a certain sempai not merely in
regard to the senior's present position but also for that person's

potential. Behavioral researchers have observed that if our treatment of other people reflects what we would like them to become, there's an observable inclination for that to indeed happen. Therefore, if we encourage our seniors and sensei to excel by showing them our respect, they might grow into leaders we can genuinely admire. At the same time, of course, the sensei and sempai are expected to take a similar respectful approach in guiding the behavior of their kohai.

An additional correlation can be seen between the sempai-kohai relationship and the parent-child connection. Parents who constantly tell their children they will amount to nothing often produce individuals severely limited in their ability to develop, whereas the unconditional love and devotion of a child has in some cases influenced parents away from everything from crime to alcohol addiction.

Readers who have lived in Japan and seen the sempai-kohai system in action know that it doesn't always resemble a healthy parent-child relationship; frequent abuses by seniors take place in Japan, and mistreatment of kohai and deshi takes place even in the Ways. Nonetheless, any system, whether it's the sempai-kohai relationship, reigi in the Ways, or a form of government, is only as good as the people who participate in it. While the Way of the universe is one, the individual Do and their forms of relating and etiquette are human expressions of this Way, and as such, they are susceptible to human frailties.

The Sensei

The word "sensei" is made up of two parts that translate literally as "born" (sei) and "before" (sen). In practice, it is used as a designation of respect in reference to someone who, by virtue of

183

Taiko

A Japanese drumming style. While taiko drums have been used for over 1,400 years, the style best known today began in the 1950s. Reputedly, one of the first uses of taiko was as a battlefield tool—to intimidate the enemy and to signal troops. Taiko were also used in the opening ceremonies of the Todaiji Buddhist temple in the eighth century, and they were incorporated into imperial court music as well. Taiko drums continue to find a place in religious observances, both Buddhist and Shinto. The modern-day taiko drum troupe, sometimes organized as a collective where the performers live under the same roof, is a relatively new development whose popularity has spread outside of Japan.

greater experience and expertise in an art, for example, has attained a high level of mastery. The appellation is used in place of the ordinary honorific suffix *-san*, as in Yamamoto-san, which then becomes Yamamoto Sensei. One's sempai can be designated as a teacher, and in that case that individual is always addressed using Sensei. Furthermore, since a Do is a Way of life, sensei are normally called so even outside the dojo, and failing to do so is to practice the Way superficially, in isolation. Regular and correct use of Sensei is another important aspect of reigi.

At the same time, sensei and sempai must also observe correct reigi and take responsibility for helping their juniors and students. For this reason, exhausted sempai sometimes feel that their position of seniority is more a curse than a privilege. Correctly fulfilling the role of sempai means more than barking orders at those who are less experienced and demands giving serious attention to the growth and development of one's juniors, which is not an easy task.

Some students might wonder why the Do ask that they show respect for others through bowing, the use of titles, and other outward actions. They might believe that feeling a certain way toward another is sufficient, or that this attitude need not be visibly demonstrated. However, a student learns more effectively in an atmosphere that engenders respect for the teacher and the seniors. Reigi links the atmosphere of respect and those within that atmosphere, and in this way it brings an element of seriousness to the practice of the art that is beneficial. It encourages the sensei to be devoted to his students' welfare and students to show sincere respect to the sensei and the practice. This "vertical attitude" has proven effective for transmitting an ancient discipline from one generation to the next. In addition, the goal in pursuing a Way is a synchronization of mind and body: thoughts and actions should be one. Therefore, it is natural that students should bow and say

"Thank you, Sensei" to their teacher after receiving instruction. By physically showing gratitude at the moment it is felt and by expressing feelings aloud, students experience an integration of the mind and body, a harmony of belief and action. Over time, as they practice mind and body coordination in a given Way, this behavior and mind-body harmony carry over into their lives, which is indeed the ultimate aim of practicing a Way.

Self-discipline and Nyunanshin

Reigi can be considered forms of discipline. In fact, all Do are indeed disciplines and processes of strengthening ourselves spiritually and physically. But the nature of this "discipline" isn't necessarily what might be assumed. Discipline is not necessary to eat regularly, go to the bathroom, or step out of the way of a speeding truck because we clearly see the need for these actions. What if we just as clearly saw the necessity of the Way itself? This is an essential question for deshi of the Do. If we realize the value of what we're engaged in, that it relates to the very essence of living itself, discipline becomes unnecessary.

Assuming that our sensei is a sincere, competent, and compassionate person, why might we come to think of practice as overly demanding or difficult? Could it have to do with our failure to understand the real purpose and value of the training? I think this is often the case, and although we may understand this intellectually, genuine understanding comes through direct experience with the Way. So, if we participate in a Do, is our recognition of its purpose and value wholehearted or just conceptual? Many people might not even be able to tell the difference between the two. To rephrase the question, do we understand the Way in the manner that we know fire burns or that we need water to survive? This

Taoism

Taoism is based on the Chinese concept of the Tao, represented by a single written character that can mean a "road" or "path" or, in its spiritual context, the "Way." Taoism is known as Dokyo in Japan, and this same character is the "Do" used in the names of the Japanese Ways. Taoist teachings represent the outgrowth of a Chinese heritage of nature veneration and divination. The Tao was interpreted as the origin of all creations and the life power behind all action in nature. While both the Way and its power are beyond the limits of intellectual understanding, they can nevertheless be observed in the endless manifestations of nature, where they can foster a spiritual approach to being.

Tate Shakai

"Vertical [or class] society," comparable to the relationship between a parent and child; it defines relationships between employer and employee, teacher and student—virtually all relationships in Japan. Ideally, it is not so much a system of strict hierarchical relationships as it is one of mutual service and duty and patronage and respect, alternating from one level to the other and back again. See also kobai; sempai.

question is important for people who participate in the Ways of Japan as spiritual paths. Because, with a profound recognition of its purpose and value, the need for externally imposed discipline dissolves. All discipline becomes self-discipline, but there is no sense of force; our manner of interacting with a Way is one of *choosing to participate.* In sincerely making this choice, we naturally focus ki on the completion of necessary tasks. To do less makes no sense. And one of the valuable aspects of the Ways is the opportunity to discover the true meaning of sincerity, in all aspects of living. To be sincere is to live wholeheartedly.

Our sempai have more experience and have realized an appreciation of the benefits inherent in following the Way, and, because they care about us, they want us to realize these benefits. As kohai, we in turn do our best to participate wholeheartedly. We will then someday be able to repay the kindness of our sensei in the form of our own teaching and contributions to the Way, thereby forming a circle of harmony.

We have voluntarily chosen a Way. This entails certain obligations, but they are obligations to us as much as to our sempai and sensei. If the obligations and their fulfillment are seen as a problem, it lies in thinking of an obligation as a sacrifice, a sacrifice we're making for some future, abstract gain. But the Way exists now. Its benefits are realized in what we're doing right now. It isn't something we do for the future, and its value is realized in the moment and during the training itself. Without this understanding, practice becomes a "sacrifice" we make toward a future goal. But the future might never come; the value of the Way exists in this instant. A Do as a Way of life is of immense usefulness and is worth following for its own sake.

In order to train effectively, we must be willing to change. A fixed image of oneself or a strong ego can, however, obstruct a willingness to change and grow. The Way lies in continual transformation, and reigi helps us to transcend the ego and achieve a humble, open-minded state that makes real growth possible. This state is *nyunanshin*, or "pliable mind," and it is an essential component of all the Do. Just as stretching is less painful when we "relax into the stretch," so too is spiritual growth easier when we transcend the ego and open our mind. This is nyunanshin.

Nyunanshin requires harmony with the sensei, the training, and the dojo. It is to become one with the teacher, who at that point is free to go beyond superficial teaching. Such harmony and union come from a deep sensitivity to others, particularly our sensei. They come from first emptying yourself in order to become full. This emptying, which relates to reigi, is an ongoing, lifelong process. Through the discipline that comes from freely choosing to follow the Way and the pliant, open mind of nyunanshin, we discover the true meaning and value of the Ways as spiritual practice.

On and Giri

To further understand reigi, the Ways, and their cultural context, we must consider the concepts of *on* and *giri*. On refers to "obligations" people have to one another. This feeling of being obliged or owing honor or gratitude to someone can apply to anyone, but it is particularly important in relation to ancestors, parents, seniors, and teachers. Reigi is one means of expressing to them our appreciation.

Giri describes the debts incurred to one's *onjin*, or "benefactors." Giri can mean "code of personal responsibility," "loyalty," or "duty." Each dojo position has its own giri; indeed, this is an important tradition in the Japanese arts and Ways. In Japan, giri to acquaintances is repaid according to the value of the on received;

Temari

Decorative stitched balls usually given as a present. A thousand-year-old handicraft that has its roots in balls for children, temari produces an enchanting effect on observers. As a decorative focal point, the pattern is hypnotic. The theory is simple; the result refined. Stitches go in every direction—up and down, side to side, and diagonally— because of the random wrapped thread exterior of the ball. It's been said that if you can fold a paper ribbon into halves, fourths, and eighths, you can learn temari.

Tsuba

The hand guard fixed on a Japanese sword. It kept the hand from shifting up onto the cutting edge, offset the weight of the blade, made known the social status, philosophy, and tastes of its possessor, and safeguarded the hand from a rival's sword. Tsuba are still made from metals such as copper and its alloys (brass, bronze, and others) as well as silver, gold, iron, and other metals. Many have surface texturing, cutout openwork, or inlay/overlay of different metals. The style varies with time, locale, and the imaginativeness of the artisan. Tsuba are regarded as works of art and collected throughout the world.

giri to nature, ancestors, parents, and sensei is sometimes understood as *gimu*, which refers to the sense that the duty and gratitude are ongoing. Recognizing on and giri sustains balance in nature and in relationships.

Giri is more than a codified means of preventing the shirking of unpleasant duties, though it occasionally degenerates to only that; it describes a sense of duty based on loyalty, which in turn is an outgrowth of compassion. In fact, compassion is the essence of loyalty. Both compassion and loyalty are a natural expression of the realization of humanity's interconnections and its unity with the universe. In this way, giri becomes something we embody and not just an idea we subscribe to.

Giri also offers, in the dojo and in life generally, a way to find the balance between individual self-determination and responding to group needs. This balance is essential, for we are not entirely self-sufficient and so must work with others, and yet we must realize our full potential alone if we are to truly benefit others. We are not one, not two.

Finally, giri is the mark of a sincere deshi. A good example of this kind of deshi is Yamaoka Tesshu, who lived during the mid-nineteenth century and was a master of meditation, calligraphy, and the sword. The tale is told that when Yamaoka was a young student he studied under a teacher in Edo noted for his great prowess. Not long after Yamaoka began his practice, however, his sensei met with a tragic death. Following the teacher's death came reports of a strange apparition lingering near his grave on stormy nights. One rainy, lightning-filled night, the teacher's brother was sent to determine the truth of these rumors. As he neared the grave, he noticed a figure on its knees in the mud and heard it saying, "I'm here, Sensei. Don't be afraid. I'll stay with you until the storm is over." That figure was Yamaoka.

Despite the master's prowess, he was afraid of lightning.

Yamaoka's giri transcended even the barrier of death, but, perhaps most important, he was able to accept his sensei's fears and weaknesses.

This is an important point. Western students tend toward extremes regarding their sensei—he or she is either godlike in infallibility or just one of the gang. Both are misperceptions. The bona fide sensei expresses the Way of the universe through a human form and a particular art, complete with all that being human entails.

In association with giri is the concept of *ninjo*. Ninjo means "human feelings," which take precedence over rules or profit. Teachers can change the rules affecting how a student is taught according to ninjo. My sensei often remind me that they teach "according to the student." What is appropriate for one student may not be for another.

Related to giri and ninjo is *tsukiai*, or "social debt." Students of the Ways traditionally showed tsukiai by providing their sensei with food, shelter, and whatever else was needed for the teacher's well-being. This is no longer common, having been replaced by a "tuition system" of sorts, but it is not unheard of or inappropriate.

Humility

The spirit of respect and service contained in concepts such as reigi and tsukiai underlies real learning in the Ways. True understanding comes from an immediate, unclouded perception of reality, and a learning mind is empty, empty of preconceived ideas about an art, its instruction, and acquisition. Such an unclouded, empty mind relates to humility.

Learning a Way takes time and sometimes requires a restructuring of lifestyle and habits. In order to make such changes and

Ukiyo-e

"Pictures of the floating world," a style of printmaking that started in the cosmopolitan culture of eighteenth-century Edo (Tokyo), when bureaucratic and military power was in the hands of the shogun and the nation was secluded from the world. Ukiyo-e relateds to the pleasures of theatres, restaurants, geisha, and courtesans in a bustling commercial atmosphere. Numerous ukiyo-e woodblock prints were in fact posters announcing theatre performances and brothels, or portraits of actors and teahouse girls. This more or less modern world of urban pleasures was also animated by the love of nature, and ukiyo-e artists like Hokusai had an influence on landscape painting worldwide.

Ura

Back or inside. Refers to what is invisible, not readily apparent, and in the context of human relations, relates to a "hidden face." With its counterpart, omote (front, outside, public), it speaks of a dualism in the arts of Japan and the visible-invisible, in-yo nature of the universe. See also omote.

take the time needed to acquire skill, a student must have a certain amount of perseverance. Many students, however, give up the Way too easily, believing that a lack of immediate growth indicates there is something wrong with the Way itself. A deshi with an attitude of humility realizes the fault is likely not with the training but with one's self. Through reigi, we can cultivate humility necessary for perseverance. Ultimately, however, understanding the Way is to enter into a state that transcends time, a state with no past and no future: *naka-ima*, the eternal now.

Remaining humble and persevering bring positive results. Bowing and other expressions of reigi relate not only to humbleness but also to respecting our seniors' differences and styles of teaching; different instructors teach differently, but each may still follow the Way. The unclouded, empty mind of humility recognizes this fact.

Just as one learns to be a good student, one learns to be a good instructor. These two roles are opposite sides of the same coin. The respect that kohai feel toward their sempai and sensei should be reflected in the way that sempai and sensei are aware of and respond to the needs of the kohai. In the Ways, we help those below us, while we respect those above us. Those who are kohai, if they continue, will become sempai and perhaps sensei. Sincere deshi, practicing with a qualified sensei, are rarely frozen in a single role but are simultaneously kohai, sempai, and sensei depending on the situation. They don't exist within a rigid and one-dimensional class structure. Like life, the Japanese arts and Ways are multidimensional.

Bowing and Seiza

Bowing is an expression of reigi in the classical Ways. It

must not be done in a meek and inhibited manner. It is *not* a subservient act. A correct bow reflects the respect for all creation that
lies at the heart of the Do, and it stems from a deep confidence in
our essential unity. (This is valid despite the fact that it isn't
always performed this way in Japan.) It should be done with great
dignity, for only the truly confident can bow correctly. Western
students of traditional Japanese arts who are afraid that bowing
will make them weak and subservient are already weak. Their
resistance is a reflection of what they bring to the study of the
Way in the form of past biases, conditioning, and fear. And this
sort of fear in the form of resistance is also evident outside the Do.
How often is our reaction to certain situations based on fear,
though hidden behind the guise of something else? This is a vital
question for exponents of the Do, indeed for anyone. A mind
caught in fear, and therefore in the past from which fear originates
can delude itself in vast and intricate ways.

But the power of the Way takes us beyond illusions. Deshi
manifest this power through caring and politeness. "Politeness"—
only an approximate rendering of rei—is not simply taking pains
to exhibit "good manners." Unfeigned reigi is instead the sincere
and outward expression of compassion and respect. Forms of
politeness and etiquette practiced in the Do echo a true harmony
with the natural order. The attitude characterizing these forms is
the same that has made the seemingly simple task of preparing tea
into an art and spiritual discipline.

Since bowing is a common expression of reigi in the Ways,
its correct execution must be considered. When properly performed, a bow can be a means of practicing the coordination of
mind and body that is universally valued in the Do. Bowing is
done from one of two positions: standing, *tachi-rei*, or seated, *za-
rei*. Za-rei is more formal, and each Do may have slightly different
customs relating to these two ways of bowing. The depth of the

Wabi

*An aesthetic ideal that
strongly resists easy
definition. In wabi art
we find beauty with a
feeling of austerity.
Wabi is the recogni-
tion that beauty can be
found informally, even
in the depths of pover-
ty. Objects of great
refinement can often be
constructed out of sim-
ple, inexpensive mate-
rials. A classical
Japanese wooden
house is an example of
the unpolished appeal
of wabi.*

Waka

Classical Japanese poetic form comprising five lines of five, seven, five, seven, and seven syllables, respectively. Waka themes center on the poet's feelings toward natural beauty and human emotion.

bow and the duration it is held will also vary depending on the situation. A deeper, longer-held bow is more formal.* In essence, however, the bow doesn't vary much, and what follows is a general explication of tachi-rei and za-rei. The specifics can be discovered through discussions with sempai and careful observation. The following explanation is based on the arts I'm familiar with.

Tachi-rei starts with an erect stance in which the forehead and lower abdomen are aligned, a confident posture that "looks big." The heels are near each other, with the toes pointing outward at a forty-five-degree angle, which is more stable than placing the feet together. The mind and gaze are directed straight ahead.

Keeping the alignment between the forehead and abdomen, imagine that the hara is a hinge and bow forward. As you do, slide your fingertips along your thighs in coordination with the movement of your body. The bow stops when your fingertips reach the top of your kneecaps. (This is a good "all-purpose bow," but, depending on the situation, the bow may be deeper or more shallow.) Move from your hara, which means uniting the motion of your sliding hands with your body. Graceful, unified action that centers on the hara is the standard means of movement in everything from chado to budo. Our hara coordinates the upper and lower body in a way that allows us to gracefully manifest our full power in a number of activities, and bowing correctly is one means of training movement from the hara.

Some novices bend near their solar plexus and chest when they bow, thus rounding the back and destroying their aligned posture. Others bow while looking at the person receiving the bow, which bends the head backward and out of alignment. Not only does bowing in this way move the body in opposition to the

---

* You can learn about the social and cultural aspects of bowing and reigi through a Way that focuses on the practice of traditional reigi: the Ogasawara Ryu. Check their Web site at http://www.ogasawara-ryu.com/.

eyes and mind but it is also
viewed as being impolite and
showing distrust. Letting the
head droop and thus exposing
the back of the neck also
shows a lack of coordination.
It is effective to bow as if your
head and hara were connected
(Figure 22). Pause at the bottom of the bow, then rise,
bringing the gaze up with the
body. If the body rises while
the gaze remains on the floor,
it suggests that the body is

FIG. 22. Tachi-rei, a
standing bow.

ahead of the mind, since the mind follows the eyes and vice versa.
And rising before the other person rises from her or his bow is
impolite. When in doubt, move at the same time as the other person, which, since you're looking down, requires sensitivity to your
environment and the ki of the other.

In sum, a correct bow involves the alignment of the forehead
and hara as well as of the mind and body. Acting in harmony with
the actions of others is also important. Bowing incorrectly, however, cultivates a habit of moving inefficiently while losing unity of
mind and body. Thus, proper bowing cultivates the ability to move
in a coordinated manner from the hara and harmony of mind and
body, both of which are useful in the Ways and in life.

Za-rei is done while in seiza. Sit lightly on your heels with an
erect posture. Men leave a space of about two or three fists
between their knees; women need leave a gap roughly equal to one
fist wide. Rest the hands gently at mid-thigh with the fingers
pointed slightly inward and with space between the arms and
body. Moving the gaze, mind, and body as one, bend from the hara

FIG. 23. Za-rei, a seated bow.

as you slide your hands along your thighs and to the floor in front of you. Your hands touch the floor silently and lightly, with the fingers together and the thumb and index finger of each hand forming a triangle. Aside from being elegant, this focuses ki toward the person or place you're bowing to. The forehead is generally aligned with the hara, and it should be over your triangle, about two fists from the floor. The hips stay down and the back is fairly straight (Figure 23). This might seem simple, but bending from the hara while keeping the head, neck, back, and pelvis aligned without letting the buttocks rise much from the heels requires flexibility. Za-rei and tachi-rei cultivate and sustain excellent posture and flexibility, especially in the lower back and the pelvis.

Pause after lowering the head, then rise from your hara, sliding the hands in reverse along the floor and thighs while bringing the gaze and mind up with the body. Don't rest your palms heavily on the floor, and avoid pushing off the floor as you rise: move from the hara. Resting too much weight on the hands causes tension in the shoulders and produces a "top-heavy" condition that is unstable and that subtly alters your alignment.

Flexibility, excellent posture, sensitivity to others, unification of mind and body—these benefits of the art of bowing as an expression of reigi are available to people of any culture.

Understanding the meaning and functions of reigi is important for Western students of the arts and Ways. The reticence of Japanese teachers to explain about reigi and the consequent ignorance of their Western students can lead Western deshi to think of reigi as simply social customs and, in some cases, to resent this aspect of their practice. It is important that teachers offer explanations that at least give students an idea of the why or how of reigi and other elements of the Way. In that regard, I hope that this book will prove useful not just to novices but to their teachers, who have the task of translating the Way.

Inside a Dojo

To provide an idea of how a traditional dojo functions, I offer below a scenario based on my experiences with various sensei. While some of my teachers are conservative in approach, others are more westernized. How I relate to a sensei depends on the art, its traditions, and his or her interpretation of reigi. Although the specifics vary from sensei to sensei, the essence of the Way does not.

The sensei here is modeled after me and several of my teachers, and the "I" in the story is based on me, my students, and other deshi I've known. Because my dojo is traditional in atmosphere, the nature of training is exacting and conservative. Being exposed to this, however, is to your advantage: you'll rarely have problems in Japanese culture and arts from being "too polite," but you most likely will if you are impolite. The worst that can happen if you're too polite is that your sensei will tell you to lighten up, and this

Washi

Perhaps the thinnest, toughest, and most lasting of all hand-made papers. It is also praised for its beautiful, delicate appearance and appreciated as high-level folk art. The secret of washi's durability lies in the natural material and the papermaking procedure. An unusual trait of washi paper-making is the application of bast fibers from three shrubs used as raw material. It's fabricated through a laborious and complicated process. Western-style paper is used throughout Japan, but traditional washi remains essential for specific artistic purposes and inseparable from Japanese culture. Its soft, durable attributes are unique, and its beauty has brought wide acknowledgment.

Yugen

Something cloudy or mysterious. Yet this "cloudiness" isn't out and out darkness but a state beyond the limits of thought . . . yet not beyond the capacity of human experience. We can feel yugen in great art as a kind of ineffable sensibility that resonates out from the work to captivate our moods and emotions. Each viewer and participant who has experienced yugen will identify it, but each person's experience of it is unique.

can be taken as a compliment. A rule of thumb in case of doubt or confusion is to watch your sempai's behavior, or, if you're still unsure, ask the sempai what to do. Avoid asking your sensei questions about reigi; this creates an awkward situation since such questions are often about how you should behave toward him or her. (But if you do get stuck, asking your sensei is unavoidable.)

It's Monday and I know I won't make it to practice on Tuesday. I leave a message on Sensei's answering machine to let him know not to expect me. This helps him anticipate who he'll be teaching Tuesday and, therefore, what to teach as well. Since I can't come to practice, I make a point of training on my own Tuesday evening.

It's Thursday, another practice day. I leave for the dojo a little early, allowing time so I don't have to worry about being late. Since I arrive early, I see Sensei pulling up in his Toyota. I greet him, open the car door, and help him carry a package to the dojo.

I get to the dojo door ahead of him and execute a standing bow as I enter. I greet the other deshi. I put the package down and hold the door open for Sensei. The practice area is covered with Japanese-style tatami mats, and so I remove my shoes before stepping on them. After placing my shoes in the designated spot, I step onto the mats and perform another standing bow toward the kamiza, a place of honor that houses the dojo shrine. I carry Sensei's package into the office, bowing again before I leave the practice area. Leaving Sensei, I visit the toilet to avoid having to go during class. Following this, I bow as I step into the practice area, and I join the other deshi, who are sitting in a line waiting for Sensei to start practice.

We sit in seiza. Everyone is silent. The deshi who arrived before me have cleaned the dojo. (The more things Sensei has to do, the less time he has to focus on what he's going to teach and the less time he has to teach it. *Soji*, cleaning the dojo, helps us as much as it does Sensei.) None of us speaks or moves as we calm and clear our minds to fully concentrate on the coming instruction.

Sensei walks to a spot in front of the kamiza. He sits in seiza, and we bow toward the kamiza en masse, paying respect to the spirit of the art we practice and to the generations of teachers who have paved the Way for us. Sensei turns. Still sitting in seiza, he and the deshi bow together.

He explains what will be practiced that evening. During his explanation, my legs grow tired, and I bow and sit cross-legged, sustaining an erect, alert posture. Every moment in the Ways is meditation.

The lecture is over, the instruction has been presented, and I sit in seiza again. We bow from seiza in acknowledgment of the instruction we have received. Standing up, we practice. Sensei notices me making a mistake and offers a correction. At his conclusion, I bow and say, "Thank you, Sensei." Nothing forced him to help me, and I'm grateful for the attention.

Not long thereafter, he claps his hands, signaling that he would like to move on. We form lines once again, sit in seiza, listen, and watch. Despite having visited the bathroom earlier, I need to go again. I raise my hand, indicate my need, and, with a quick bow, head off to the bathroom.

When I return, I see everyone is working in pairs. My sempai fills me in on what's going on. I find a person to practice with, and standing about six feet apart, we make a standing bow to each other. Our practice begins. After five minutes, we hear Sensei's clap, step apart, bow, and say to each other, "Thank you." This pattern continues throughout practice.

Later, while Sensei is presenting group instruction again, he asks me to assist him. I bow, rise from seiza, and move quickly to

Zanshin

Zan means "lingering," "remaining," and connotes continuation, while *shin* is simply "mind." Refers to the moment following an action, seen, for example, in a sumi-e painter's continuing movement of the brush even after it has left the paper, or in a martial artist's freezing of movement after the execution of a final stroke of the sword or jujutsu throw; the "lingering" allows the movement of ki to continue. As students of the Ways practice, they discover that stillness is as important as activity, and not doing as essential as doing, and that the moment following an action determines the success of the action and the success of any that follow.

*help him with the point he's illustrating. During this demonstra-
tion, he begins to talk. I retreat a few feet and sit in seiza. I rise
again to help him with another point, and we're done. Before
returning to my place, I bow from where I'm standing and say,
"Thank you, Sensei." I'm ready for more practice . . . but first I
look around to see if any of my kohai appear lost and in need of a
more experienced person to work with.*

*At the end of practice, Sensei and the deshi sit again, facing
the kamiza. A seated bow is performed, Sensei turns, and we all
bow, saying, "Thank you, Sensei." Instruction is over. Sensei says
"Thank you" as well. It was hot, so I bring him water and ask a
question or two while I have his attention. I know better than to
assume someone else will take care of such things. Maybe they
will, maybe they won't. The dojo teaches us to take matters into
our own hands.*

*Later, Sensei prepares to leave, while the deshi make sure the
dojo lights are off, doors closed, etc. I help him with his jacket
and place his shoes where he can easily step into them. Opening
the door for him, the other deshi and I wish him good night. I
bow again toward the kamiza, and as I'm about to leave, I say
"Goodnight" to the remaining deshi. We always acknowledge
each other and extend our good-byes, because we realize that our
dojo must function harmoniously—and the deshi are the dojo.*

From this example of practice in a dojo, you can see there is
much to remember and a great deal of bowing. But the bowing and
other forms of respect have a purpose beyond politeness and gratitude. Students have a lot to remember, and they can't, therefore,
absentmindedly blunder through practice. Ongoing awareness is
needed, and reigi helps students stay focused on what they're
doing and serves as a constant reminder of why they started practice to begin with. Reigi acts as an outward barometer of whether

or not we're awake during practice. It also helps us understand Japanese culture on more than a theoretical level, which allows us to comfortably interact with Japanese people or function in Japan. In short, reigi is cross-cultural education of a concrete nature.

The integral place of respect, gratitude, and compassion in the Do provides us a unique opportunity to truly consider their meaning and value. This opportunity is one of the functions of reigi. Reigi also allows us to demonstrate tangibly, with our whole mind and body, the essence of the heart. This wholeheartedness as an expression of reigi is called *kokoro ire* (*kokoro*, "mind/spirit/heart"; *ire*, "to put in"). Kokoro ire in the Ways takes chado and kado, for example, beyond merely sipping tea and putting flowers on display. What reigi and its expressions cultivate, then, is constant awareness, cross-cultural understanding, respect, gratitude, and compassion, and these are qualities of value to anyone, regardless of cultural background.

An International Aesthetic of the Way

The arts and Ways of Japan are being studied and taught in many places outside Japan, and as a result they are continually evolving. Successfully transmitting a practice to a new culture, however, requires an intimate understanding of its native cultural context and also an understanding of the non-Japanese students of the art. Westerners, for example, thus have a responsibility to know deeply an art and its Japanese cultural home before attempting to alter or adapt that art in a new, Western setting. Japanese sensei, if they desire the integrity of their arts to be preserved in their transmission to Americans or Europeans, must make an attempt to understand Western students. From this mutual understanding a new international aesthetic can grow and develop.

Through the traditional Japanese arts and Ways, all of us have a chance to realize not only a unification of mind and body but also a unity of East and West, as well as a union of humanity with the Way of the universe. In this ultimate unification, the Do and the deshi become one, shining so brightly that all living things are illuminated.

MU

FINDING A SENSEI

Having come this far, you are probably interested in proceeding further and are ready to search for a skilled instructor. This appendix offers assistance in finding a sensei and additional information about the Japanese arts and Ways.

The Sennin Foundation Center for Japanese Cultural Arts

Founded by me in 1981, the Sennin Foundation Center for Japanese Cultural Arts offers traditional instruction in a number of the Japanese Ways. Of primary importance to its students is the study of Shin-shin-toitsu-do, a form of Japanese yoga. If you are interested in practicing the mind-body exercises found in chapter 3 (as well as other aspects of Japanese yoga), please get in touch with us. Below you'll find contact information as well as an introduction to what we have to offer.

The Sennin Foundation Center
for Japanese Cultural Arts
P. O. Box 5447
Richmond, CA 94805
E-MAIL: hedavey@aol.com

WEB SITE: www.michionline.org/ sennin-center/

JAPANESE YOGA

The main area of study at the Sennin Foundation Center is Shin-shin-toitsu-do. This art, inspired by the teachings of Nakamura Tempu Sensei, its founder, includes stretching exercises, seated meditation, moving meditation, breathing exercises, healing arts, and health improvement methods. The goal is the realization of one's full potential in everyday life through unification of mind and body.

In 1919, Nakamura Sensei, upon returning from studying yoga in India, began to share with others universal principles and exercises that could be adopted by all people regardless of age, sex, or cultural background. Nakamura Sensei placed importance on methods with observable and repeatable results and on principles and exercises that could withstand objective scrutiny.

He identified certain qualities that people need in order to meaningfully express themselves in life:

Tai-ryoku: "the power of the body," physical strength, health, and endurance

Tan-ryoku: "the power of courage"

Handan-ryoku: "the power of decision," good judgment

Danko-ryoku: "the power of determination," willpower for resolute and decisive action

Sei-ryoku: "the power of vitality," energy or life power for endurance and perseverance

No-ryoku: "the power of ability," the capacity for wide-ranging ability and dexterous action

Most important, Nakamura Sensei realized that the mind and body are our most fundamental tools, and in order to effectively express ourselves in life, we must use these tools naturally and in coordination with each other. It is this ability to effectively use and unite our minds and bodies that allows for freedom of action and skilled self-expression. Nakamura Sensei conceived a set of basic principles by which people could discover how to unite mind and body.

Using his background in Western medicine (he obtained a medical degree in the United States), Nakamura Tempu Sensei conducted biological research dealing with the nervous system and the unification of mind and body. The result was his Four Basic Principles to Unify Mind and Body. These are:

1. Use the mind positively.
2. Use the mind with full concentration.
3. Use the body obeying the laws of nature.
4. Train the body progressively, systematically, and regularly.

HEALING ARTS

Nakamura Sensei also taught self-healing and bodywork (*hitori ryoho* or self-massage). He emphasized *yuki*, which is the transference of life energy through a massagelike technique.

In life, it's important to throw 100 percent of ourselves into the moment at hand, and this positive mental state is called *ki no dashikata*, or "the projection of life energy." When our life energy freely exchanges with the life energy that pervades nature, we're in our happiest and healthiest state. We've all met exceptionally positive and animated individuals, people who project a "large presence." The intangible but unmistakable "big presence" such people project can be thought of as universal life energy, which is, as you now know, called ki in Japanese.

A relaxed body and positive mental state set this energy free, whereas physical tension and/or the negative use of the mind cause a withdrawal and loss of ki. Yuki functions in a way not dissimilar to a blood transfusion and "transfuses" this universal life energy. By studying methods of mind-body coordination and Shin-shin-toitsu-do meditation, it is possible to learn to transfer ki from the thumbs, fingertips, and palms to weakened parts of the body as a way of boosting the natural healing process. Students at the Sennin Foundation Center can receive instruction in this unique art of healing.

MARTIAL ARTS

The Sennin Foundation Center also has an aiki-jujutsu division. Jujutsu is Japan's oldest martial art. The warriors of ancient Japan used it for predominantly empty-handed combat. Aiki-jujutsu is a system that can be traced to the Aizu clan's Nisshinkan training hall in present-day Fukushima. It was taught in modern times by Saigo Tanomo Sensei (1829–1905), an Aizu clan elder adviser. Saigo Sensei taught aiki-jujutsu, formerly known as Aizu *oshikiuchi*, to Takeda Sokaku Sensei (1860–1943), disseminator of the famed Daito Ryu aiki-jujutsu system, who in turn taught Ueshiba Morihei Sensei (1883–1969), the founder of aikido.

My late father started studying jujutsu and Kodokan judo in 1926. After twenty years of training, he was stationed in Japan following World War II. While there he studied Saigo Ryu systems of aiki-jujutsu, *jojutsu* ("art of the four-foot stick"), *bojutsu* ("art of the six-foot staff"), *hanbojutsu* ("art of the three-foot stick"), *tanbojutsu* ("art of the fourteen-inch stick"), *tessenjutsu* ("art of the

iron fan"), *juttejutsu* ("art of the forked metal truncheon"), *sojutsu* ("art of the spear"), and *kenjutsu* ("art of the sword"). He later became the first American to receive the advanced rank/title of Nihon Jujutsu Kyoshi from Japan's prestigious Kokusai Budoin, a worldwide martial arts federation established in Tokyo over fifty years ago. He was also a black belt in judo and aikido.

I began aiki-jujutsu at the age of five and studied judo and aikido. I've trained in Japan and the United States and have received the positions of U.S. Branch Director for the Kokusai Budoin and Councilor to the Kokusai Budoin World Headquarters.

I emphasize aiki-jujutsu as a noncompetitive art with roots in Japan's traditional past. Like aikido, aiki-jujutsu is based on aiki, or "union with ki." Aiki-jujutsu, however, contains a wider variety of unarmed and armed techniques than is found in most forms of aikido. These skills encompass throwing and pinning methods using all parts of the body, including the feet, plus close-distance and ground grappling, and a broad range of weapons.

Since aiki-jujutsu involves harmonizing with ki, it can transform the lives of its participants. This transformation does not take place only in the realm of dynamic self-protection. Owing to the unique characteristics of aiki-jujutsu, it is possible to experience enhanced calmness, relaxation, concentration, willpower, and physical fitness in daily living. Details of this martial art can be found in my book, *Unlocking the Secrets of Aiki-jujutsu.*

FINE ARTS

The Sennin Foundation Center also has a fine arts division that emphasizes the unification of mind and body by practicing traditional Japanese fine arts.

The Center's brush writing class stresses calligraphy, but it also includes ink painting and the study of haiku and waka poetry. Expanded attention, deeper relaxation, increased focus and resolve—students have a chance to achieve spiritual transformation through the classical art of calligraphy. Simple step-by-step exercises let beginners and nonartists alike work with brush and ink to reveal their mental and physical states through moving brush meditation.

Kanji, or Chinese characters, have transcended their utilitarian function and serve as a visually stirring fine art. Shodo allows the dynamic movement of the artist's spirit to become observable in the form of rich black ink. Many practitioners believe that the "visible rhythm" of Japanese calligraphy embodies a "picture of the mind," and calligraphers recognize that it discloses our spiritual state. This is summed up by the saying, *Kokoro tadashikereba sunawachi fude tadashii,* "If your mind is correct, the brush will be correct."

Since shodo is an art, it is not strictly necessary to be able to read Chinese characters or the phonetic scripts of *hiragana* and *katakana* to admire their dynamic beauty. Within Japanese calligraphy, we find essential elements that constitute all art: creativity, balance, rhythm, grace, and the beauty of line.

Finding a Sensei

Finding a suitable sensei is obviously paramount in achieving a successful, satisfying practice of a Way, and following are some ways that might be useful in locating a teacher:

- If a Japanese community center is nearby, check their classes.

- Sometimes colleges have classes in Japanese arts. Check their catalogs and especially night- and adult-school offerings.

- Many Buddhist churches and centers also present classes in Asian cultural arts. Look in the telephone directory for a Buddhist church.

- Try contacting the nearest Japanese consulate and asking for aid. Occasionally this can garner results.

- Talk to instructors of different Japanese arts; these sensei might be able to help you, even if they or their particular art is not what you're interested in.

- In general, get involved in the local Japanese community, as this will strengthen your awareness of all of the Japanese arts and can also open many doors.

Finding a capable teacher is rarely quick and easy. Some people have looked for several years before discovering the right sensei. Once a sensei has been found, be prepared to spend a considerable amount of time and labor in studying a specific Way. This might seem intimidating, but it is critical to realize that the effort and commitment to any Japanese art bring rewards in equal measure.

Using the World Wide Web

The Web offers a vast amount of data about an equally immense number of Japanese art forms. Unfortunately, it can also be the source of a large amount of misinformation. With that caveat in mind, undertaking a Web search can be useful. Try visiting the Web site *Michi Online: Journal of Japanese Cultural Arts*, which presents reliable resources relating to a large variety of Japanese arts and Ways. The site can be reached on the Internet at:

www.michionline.org.

A Final Word

A novice might ask if there isn't an easier way to start practicing a Japanese art or Way. Serious practitioners and teachers of any of the Ways are keenly aware of the tremendous benefits that come from the uncommon effort involved in their study. As a result, they're not always sympathetic to the novice's desire for a hasty, easy approach. A ten-easy-lesson approach to an art will bring only a very shallow understanding: meaningfulness demands serious effort.

Nonetheless, I can offer this bit of advice: be sincere, persevere, and keep your eyes, ears, and mind open. Once you find a sensei, be open-minded, maintain a good attitude, and attend class regularly. Both attitude and attendance are vital: attitude equals mind, and attendance equals body. Mind and body are of equal importance in the Ways. Attending every practice session but with a closed, resistant mind precludes learning; likewise, a sincere attitude but only sporadic attendance results in poor ability.

When I first started to study Japanese calligraphy, I had been practicing Japanese yoga and martial arts for most of my life, so I had some idea of what I needed to do to participate in a new Way. I didn't skip a single class for the initial five years. The first class I missed was when my art was being shown in Japan at the International Japanese Calligraphy Exhibition. I was in Urayasu to receive an award for my brush writing and was unable to attend practice. The second time was a few years later when my father passed away.

No matter how sincere the mind may be, if the body is unable to practice consistently under a competent sensei, progress will be slow. With the right attitude and regular attendance, a student is well on his or her Way.

NOTES & REFERENCES

1. Lao Tsu, *Tao Te Ching*, trans. Gia-Fu Feng and Jane English (New York: Vintage Books, 1972), p. 25.

2. Stephen Addis, ed., and Jane Carpenter, contrib., *Japanese Ghosts and Demons* (New York: George Braziller, 1985), p. 57.

3. Dave Lowry, "The Ways of Japan," *Michi Online: Journal of Japanese Cultural Arts* (Richmond, Calif.), Summer 1999, p. 6.

4. Michio Kushi, *The Book of Do-In: Exercise for Physical and Spiritual Development* (Tokyo: Japan Publications, 1979), p. 39.

5. E. J. Harrison, *The Fighting Spirit of Japan* (Woodstock, N.Y.: The Overlook Press, 1982), p. 155.

6. Daisetz T. Suzuki, *Zen and Japanese Culture* (Princeton, N.J.: Princeton University Press, 1970), p. 284.

7. Donald Richie, *The Donald Richie Reader: 50 Years of Writing on Japan*, ed. Arturo Silva (Berkeley, Calif.: Stone Bridge Press, 2001), p. 31.

8. Richie, *The Donald Richie Reader*, p. 31.

9. Soshitsu Sen XV, *Tea Life, Tea Mind* (New York and Tokyo: Weatherhill, 1979), p. 67.

10. Man-jan Cheng, *Lao-Tzu: "My Words Are Very Easy to Understand,"* trans. Tam C. Gibbs (Berkeley, Calif.: North Atlantic Books, 1981), p. 24.

11. Yanagi Soetsu, *The Unknown Craftsman* (Tokyo and New York: Kodansha International, 1989), p. 127.

12. Lowry, "The Ways of Japan," p. 6.

13. Kenneth Yasuda, *The Japanese Haiku* (Rutland, Vt., and Tokyo: Tuttle, 1957), pp. 30–31.

14. Yoel Hoffman, *Japanese Death Poems: Written by Zen Monks and Haiku Poets on the Verge of Death* (Rutland, Vt., and Tokyo: Tuttle, 1996), p. 68.

The following works helped in the writing of this book and may be of interest to readers.

Chamberlain, Basil Hall. *Japanese Things: Being Notes on Various Subjects Connected with Japan.* Boston: Tuttle, 1989.

de Garis, Frederic, and Atsuharu Sakai. *We Japanese*. London: Kegan Paul, 2001.

Draeger, Donn F. *Classical Budo*. Tokyo and New York: Weatherhill, 1996.

Furyu: The Online Budo Journal of Classical Japanese Martial Arts and Culture. http://www.furyu.com.

Leggett, Trevor. *A First Zen Reader*. Boston: 1980.

———. *Zen and the Ways*. Boston: Tuttle, 1987.

Lowry, Dave. *Autumn Lightning: Education of an American Samurai*. Boston: Shambhala, 2001.

———. *Moving Toward Stillness: Lessons in Daily Life from the Martial Ways of Japan*. Boston: Tuttle, 2000.

———. *Persimmon Wind: A Martial Artist's Journey in Japan*. Boston: Tuttle, 1998.

———. *Sword and Brush: The Spirit of the Martial Arts*. Boston: Shambhala, 1995.

Random, Michel. *Japan: Strategy of the Unseen*. Translated by Cyrian P. Blamires. Wellingborough, Northamptonshire, England: Crucible/Thorson's Publishing; New York: Sterling, 1987.

Slawson, David A. *Secret Teachings in the Art of Japanese Gardens*. Tokyo and New York: Kodansha International, 1991.

ABOUT THE AUTHOR

H. E. DAVEY's involvement in Japanese cultural arts started during childhood. He began studying the martial art of aiki-jujutsu at the age of five under his late father, who had trained in Japan and the United States and who held certification from more than one martial arts association in Japan.

Mr. Davey is currently the highest-ranking American in the Nihon Jujutsu and Kobudo divisions of the Kokusai Budoin, a federation sponsored by the Japanese Imperial Family. He holds the rank/title of Kyoshi from the Kokusai Budoin. (Kokusai Budoin defines Kyoshi as a "Master's Certificate" and states that it is equal to a sixth- to eighth-degree black belt.) Mr. Davey is also on the board of directors of the Shudokan Martial Arts Association and is a member of the advisory board for *Furyu: The Budo Journal*.

Mr. Davey has received extensive instruction in Shin-shin-toitsu-do (The Way of Mind and Body Unification), a Japanese style of yoga founded by Nakamura Tempu Sensei in 1919. He has practiced directly under three of Nakamura Sensei's senior disciples and is currently the sole American member of the Tempu Society, an organization founded by the late Nakamura Tempu Sensei. His training in Shin-shin-toitsu-do has taken place in Japan and the United States. Mr. Davey has also received comprehensive instruction in Nakamura Sensei's methods of healing with *ki* ("life energy") and bodywork, which he teaches. His emphasis is on *yuki*, or the "transference of ki," as a way of aiding recovery from illness or injury.

Mr. Davey has studied shodo, or traditional brush writing and ink painting, under Kobara Ranseki Sensei of Kyoto. Kobara Sensei, the present Shihan (Headmaster) of the Ranseki Sho Juku system of shodo, is also the Vice President of the Kokusai Shodo Bunka Koryu Kyokai, an international shodo association headquartered in Japan. Mr. Davey holds the highest rank in Ranseki Sho Juku shodo and exhibits his artwork annually in Japan.

Mr. Davey is the President of the Sennin Foundation, which sponsors the acclaimed Internet magazine *Michi Online*. He is also the Director of the San Francisco Bay Area–based Sennin Foundation Center for Japanese Cultural Arts.

In the MICHI: JAPANESE ARTS & WAYS series, H.E. Davey explores the mind/body connection that lies at the heart of traditional Japanese arts and culture. Each volume contains lucid explanations of basic principles as well as simple exercises to help you along the Way.

STONE BRIDGE PRESS

P.O. Box 8208
Berkeley, CA 94707
1-800-947-7271
sbp@stonebridge.com

Contact your local
bookseller or shop
online

Japanese Yoga

The Way of Dynamic Meditation

The ultimate goal of Japanese yoga—or Shin-shin-toitsu-do—is enhanced mind/body integration, calmness, and willpower. This third volume in the MICHI series offers a new approach to experienced yoga students and a natural methodology that newcomers will find easy to learn. Included are seated and moving meditations, health exercises, and self-healing arts, plus effective stretching exercises, information about ongoing practice, and a glossary and reference section. Illustrated, with step-by-step discussions.

"SHIN-SHIN-TOITSU-DO HAS CHANGED MY LIFE. IT IS NOT JUST A DISCIPLINE I CAN PRACTICE IN CLASS BUT ACTUALLY PUT TO USE AT WORK, AT HOME, DRIVING MY CAR . . . IN SHORT, ANYWHERE. IT HAS PROVEN A SUBSTANTIAL BENEFIT TO MY LIFE."—DR. DOUGLAS CARY

240 pp, 7 x 9", paper, 9 brush paintings, 61 b/w instructional photos, ISBN 1-880656-60-4, $18.95

The Japanese Way of the Flower

Ikebana as Moving Meditation

WITH ANN KAMEOKA

This second MICHI volume of "moving meditations" shows how simple Japanese flower arranging (*ikebana*) techniques can be used to refresh the body and restore the spirit. Emphasizing that ikebana is first and foremost a "Way"—a spiritual and meditative art—the book offers solid grounding in Japanese aesthetics and philosophy, with references to Zen, tea ceremony, and other traditional Japanese arts. Line drawings and color photographs show step-by-step arrangements especially for beginners and casual practitioners.

"INSTRUCTS AS WELL AS INSPIRES . . . A WONDERFUL WORK THAT WILL ENRICH ANYONE'S PERSONAL WAY OF SELF-CULTIVATION."—STEPHEN M. FABIAN, PH.D., AUTHOR OF *CLEARING AWAY CLOUDS*

152 pp, 7 x 9", paper, 4 brush paintings, 32 b/w drawings, 8 pp color photos, ISBN 1-880656-47-7, $16.95

Brush Meditation

A Japanese Way to Mind & Body Harmony

Based on traditional Japanese *shodo*, "the Way of Calligraphy," *Brush Meditation*—the first volume in the MICHI series—introduces beginners and non-artists alike to working with brush and ink as a form of "moving meditation." As the text explores the intricate relationships of mind, body, and brush, it delves into the mysteries of human life energy, or *ki*, and the power of the *hara*, a natural abdominal center. Simple exercises show how to use the brush in spiritual practice, while illustrations guide every step.

"BEAUTIFULLY PRODUCED WITH GORGEOUS SAMPLES OF BRUSHWORK."—*Pathways*

144 pp, 7 x 9", paper, 4 brush paintings, 33 b/w drawings, 13 b/w instructional photos, ISBN 1-880656-38-8, $14.95

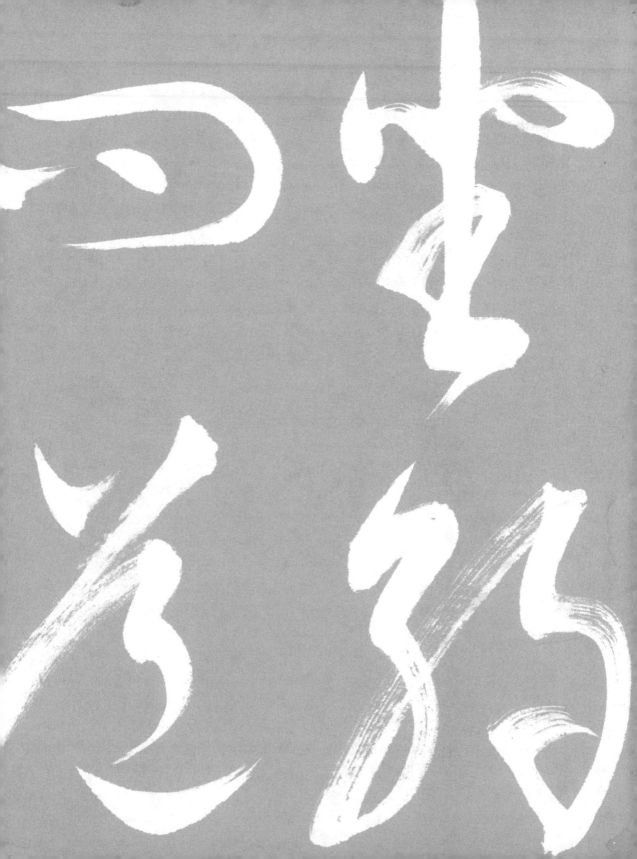